"Tommy has taken the lives of three musicians and paralleled their stories into a single encounter, that changed the face of Rock n' Roll forever. The Day the Music Died. Their story made them Rock n' Roll legends inspiring musicians everywhere. My brother Ritchie lived his dream for eight short months. Ritchie's legacy continues through his family and millions of fans around the world."

—Connie Valens, younger sister to Ritchie.

To Connie Valens! You're a beautiful soul who gave me your time, answered all my questions regardless of how easy or difficult they may have been, and just talked in general about life. Ours is a new friendship that will remain. Your brother said it best, "Blue birds over the mountain, seagulls over the sea!" God Bless!

Thank you to the Valens Family for the use of these photos!

Shadows Over Clear Lake

The Tragic Tale of the 1959 Winter Dance Party

TOMMY CANALE

Copyright © 2025 by Tommy Canale

Book Cover by Kelly Burgin of K Burgin Designs

First Edition 2025

Rella

To the generation who grew up in the era of the fifties, may this story take you back to a simpler time full of happy memories. To all the other generations, may this tale bring to life what it was like to live in the 50s but more importantly expose you to these artists and their music! It is known that stars don't fall from the sky, but the sky took our stars!

"Without Elvis, none of us could have made it"
~Buddy Holly

Table of Contents

Foreword

Somewhere, Someone is Singing

By Antonino D'Ambrosio

The car felt cold. I never liked getting in it in winter. The blue foam padded cloth and vinyl seats were stiff and rigid. This was my parent's 1971 Dodge Dart, with a powder-blue exterior and a 318 cruiser engine. My father was especially proud of that engine. For me, maybe for every kid, sitting in the back seat with my younger brother, driving around with my parents in the mid-1970s Philadelphia in that Dodge Dart, or what we called "la macchina," was as boring as watching paint dry. Very, very boring. Those trips in that cold, metal car seemed to never end. Never.

Yet in those moments where we feel stuck, there are glimpses of being free. You just have to listen—not hear but really listen for the sounds of that freedom. And that freedom for me came from the car's radio. My parents loved music. Our family loved music. And while driving around Philly, the music of Marvin Gaye, Frankie Avalon, The Temptations, Roberta Flack, The Staple Singers, The Rolling Stones, Philly's own The O'Jays, and Diana Ross would filter out of the car speakers that sounded as though they were covered in cotton but was like magic to me. Driving and listening to music. Perfect. The music from the radio was the soundtrack of the future, of my future. It vibrated with the rhythms that said life was full of possibility. Limitless. No matter the darkness, singing brings the light. It always gives us a chance to be better. To be alive. To be free.

I can't remember when I first heard Buddy Holly, but in my memories, which are a mix of my dreams and experiences, I

1

first heard him in that old Dodge Dart. It must have been when I was four or five years old. I remember my mother, who loved to dance, swaying like she was dancing in her seat next to my father in the front of the car. The song could have been "Oh Boy," "Everyday," "Not Fade Away," or "It's So Easy," because I soon came to listen to and love all of Holly's music. But in my memory, the first song was "Rave On." The title told me everything about this artist's spirit and connected me to him and the world in a visceral, emotional, hopeful way. How Holly sang the lyric "Rave on, it's a crazy feelin'" was a message aimed directly at me. Yes, the song was about love (or the intense feeling of desire), but it was about so much more: it was about being alive. It became a mantra. Rave on.

When I was young, I was so spellbound by the radio that I dreamed every song was performed live in a studio somewhere by each artist and then broadcast directly to all listening. So Billy Preston would perform "Nothing from Nothing" with his band, and then John Lennon would come out with his band and perform "Whatever Gets You Through the Night," followed by Earth, Wind and Fire performing "You're A Shining Star." And then and then and then… It was every musician everywhere. Real. Alive.

I knew this was not true since we had a house full of records constantly being played on those monstrous, giant, brown music consoles (with built-in turntables, radio, and eight-track players) that many working-class families had in their living rooms. But music is not about something as serious as reality; it's about something more important than that. It's about dreaming. So, when I found myself in Austin, Texas in March 2010 to perform at the SXSW Music Festival in support of my book A Heartbeat and a Guitar: Johnny Cash's

Bitter Tears, something pulled and pushed me to get into a car and drive over three hundred and seventy miles and more than six hours from Austin to Lubbock, Texas, Holly's hometown.

That drive and my time in Lubbock have never left me. I wanted to breathe in the same air, stand under the same Texas sky, and walk on the same Lubbock streets that Holly did while wearing those thick black glasses and carrying his Fender Stratocaster. I soon realized I had been doing that for most of my life. Listening to his music was him sharing his air, his life with me. Music makes you breathe deeply. And maybe that's the power—it continually sustains us, breathes life into us, reminds us that we're human and that we always have a chance.

This alchemy captures my connection to Tommy Canale, who has written a book filled with what it means to be alive, to be real, not just to remember but to honor, to celebrate, and to sing. When Tommy first discussed this project with me, it began as something different, one that I hope we will one day revisit. Yet, as all things that reach beyond our reality and slip into our imagination and heart do, Tommy found a deeper story to tell. And that's what this book is: something beautiful and extraordinary.

In this book, you can breathe deeply and feel Holly, his life, his death, and his ghost, which inhabits contemporary music not as a sad specter but as a sensitive saint. "There's a blaze of light in every word," Leonard Cohen sang. "It doesn't matter which you heard, the holy or the broken, hallelujah." This could be Cohen's tribute to Holly. And Tommy feels that blaze of light and infuses it in every word of this book. "So I tried to touch, I've told the truth, I didn't come to fool you,"

3

Cohen sings. Here, these lyrics describe Tommy and Holly, now united in history.

Unmatched in his research and storytelling approach, Tommy began to excavate Holly's story in an original, thrilling way that offers revelations—surprising and tragic, beautiful and sad—that present a new dimension to Holly's life and death that is much more about each of us than one of us. During the process of writing this book, Tommy's calls, emails, and text messages became more like little gifts to me as he shared with the enthusiasm and spirit of an artist breaking through the stone to find the sculpture buried inside, each and every exciting discovery and new idea to the story.

Tommy possesses a quality of living and creating in this world that few have and many seek. With an open mind and open heart, he offers stories that sink deeply into all who encounter them. Overcoming colon and liver cancer, Tommy is a survivor. His successful battle with cancer didn't lead to any epiphanies. He didn't need any. It only intensified the pursuit of living the way he always had: with compassion, curiosity, a passion to learn, and a resolute determination to connect and to be of service. This is all in Tommy's book, not just in the sentences, paragraphs, and chapters but in the empty spaces between each and every line. Tommy is the perfect storyteller to pick up Buddy Holly's story, one that is fading away, and carry it forward, handing it out to a whole new generation.

Tommy is taking up Holly's challenge to not fade away but stake a claim. For me, I see a link between Tommy and Holly's story. Maybe a link we all share. I think of poet Pablo Neruda: "You can crush the flowers, but you can't stop the spring." These words must have been written for Tommy and

Holly or any of us who experience death, loss, or tragedy of some kind. You can crush a life, but you can't stop living. It's a reminder that the power of the human spirit flows throughout our history, into our present, and gives us a chance—every day, every moment—to make the future sublime. Not fade away. Ever. But to glow brightly. Forever.

Tommy is from Streator, Illinois, with a population of just over 12,000. Like another resident of Streator, Clyde Tombaugh, who discovered the dwarf planet Pluto in 1930, Tommy had his eyes set on the stars. He looked to the sky and thought the universe was vast and, therefore, must be full of inspiring people—Tommy's 'stars'—who were waiting for him. Tommy first channeled this desire to connect with people through sports, coaching Junior College basketball and serving as an athletic director. To motivate and inspire young athletes, you must make them believe—truly believe—in themselves and each other. Tommy found the best way to do this was through storytelling, and he was a success. His teams and programs were a success. He is often heard saying, "It's not about 'I' and 'me' but about 'us' and 'we'."

Tommy, a former on-air radio personality and mobile DJ, took his love of storytelling, connecting to and with people, and found an even larger platform with his popular podcast "Before the Lights." It was broadcast and streamed in over a hundred countries. I had the privilege of being a guest on "Before the Lights" many times and then worked with Tommy on our podcast series, "A Heartbeat and a Guitar." Appearing as a guest and then producing and hosting alongside Tommy, I had the incredible privilege of seeing him work, admiring his attention to detail, fierce research, transcendent thoughtfulness, and steadfast determination.

5

Our bond grew, and with it, our support for each other's work. But underneath all of this was another passion we shared: music. It always comes back to the music, a dynamic transmitter for visceral storytelling. In this book, Tommy's imagination and creativity are completely set free, and we, the readers, are all the recipients of this gift. Perhaps, as any great artist does, Holly had been calling to Tommy throughout his life, as he had mine, through his music, the root for nearly all the popular music that floats into our ears today.

Music matters to Tommy. And the music of Buddy Holly matters. Without him, there would have been no Bob Dylan, Beatles, Rolling Stones, Johnny Cash, and the list goes on. Just ask them, and they'll tell you. "I learned from Buddy Holly how to write songs and put them together." That's Mick Jagger. "Buddy Holly was everything I wanted to be." This is Bob Dylan. "Looking back over the last twenty years, I guess the guy I've admired most in rock and roll is Buddy Holly," And this is Elvis Presley.

Holly was one of the first to craft the blueprint for the modern rock band, incorporating the electric guitar as a lead instrument and pioneering a sound that fused rock, rhythm and blues, and country. His distinct style, his crisp falsetto, his catchy melodies, and his raw energy were revolutionary. In the years since his untimely death, Buddy Holly's music has transcended the decades, forged by a legacy of innovation, passion, and, above all, the power of music to bring people together.

This book seeks to explore the life, music, and enduring impact of Buddy Holly—not just as a music legend but as someone whose talent and vision helped shape the direction of modern popular music. Tommy goes into every darkened corner, under every rock, and through every locked door to reveal the lasting imprint Holly left on both the music industry and the world. Through interviews, stories, and reflections, Tommy uncovers not just the man behind the glasses but the musician whose legacy still raves on in today's music.

In a world where trends come and go as fast as the length of a Tik-Tok video, Buddy Holly's eternal sound remains a testament to the idea that the best music, like the best stories, endures forever. You're going to learn—and feel—this and much more from Tommy's book. Get ready. So, when you hold this book in your hands, and when you read these words that Tommy Canale has written, you know that someone, somewhere, is singing.

Introduction

Thinking that one day I would be writing a book is beyond imaginary. As someone who enjoys researching but not at all writing, this is outside my comfort zone. This story, not to mention the part of history and my trip in September of 2022, has made a significant impact on me. I opened my laptop one day and without thinking about what I was doing, I started writing. I went on vacation with my mother and my sister at the end of the summer of that year. We decided to visit the Buddy Holly Memorial site and then go over to Surf Ballroom, which is where they last played. This inspired me to research this part of American history and led to "The Last Dance Party" show on my Before the Lights Podcast, which was released on February 2nd, 2023, coinciding with the date they played their last show in 1959. After receiving so much positive feedback, I kept digging into this story, which motivated me to write this book.

Please keep in mind that I am not a writer but a researcher. For some, this will be a trip down memory lane, while others will learn about three rock and roll artists and the date that has forever been known as The Day the Music Died.

Prologue

"We interrupt this program for a special news bulletin. Three young singers who soared to the heights of show business on the current rock and roll craze were killed today in the crash of a light plane in an Iowa snow flurry. The singers were identified as Ritchie Valens seventeen, Buddy Holly twentytwo, and JP Richardson twenty-eight, known professionally as The Big Bopper. The aircraft chartered from the Dwyer Flying Service crashed near Mason City, ironically the setting for the prominent musical The Music Man. The pilot Roger Peterson of Clear Lake, Iowa was also killed. The three singers had appeared at the Surf Ballroom in Clear Lake, Iowa last night and were on their way to Fargo, North Dakota. Their small, chartered plane crashed in a lonely farmyard about fifteen miles northwest of Mason City. The cause of the crash was due to inclement weather conditions. Details upcoming from Action Central News.

(Newscast recorded February 3rd, 1959-KGLO Radio, Mason City, IA).

The date was February 3rd. The plane, now fifty-four minutes late for departure, was one of the last to leave Chicago before the airport closed due to wind and blinding snow. The time was 9:54 p.m. CST. The American Airlines Flight 320 was headed for New York City's LaGuardia Airport in a twoweek-old Lockheed Electra aircraft. At 11:34 p.m. the plane was approaching the NYC area and was descending through the clouds and fog in poor weather conditions. At 11:55 p.m., flying at 160 mph and lower than the path it was supposed to be on, it crashed into the icy East River, coming up 4,900 feet short of the runway. It was complete darkness and thick fog; the rescuers could hear the cries of survivors, but the poor visibility and swift river current was making recovery extremely difficult. Nearby residents claimed they heard calls for help downstream from the crash. Sixty-five died of the seventy-five onboard, one crash victim Beulah Zachary, the executive producer of the television series "Fran and Ollie" which aired from 1947-1957. Surviving crew members said the aircraft's instruments had indicated normal altitudes right up to impact. The altimeter was the focus of the investigation, as there were different styles in older types of aircraft to this newer Electra.

The Civil Aeronautics Board claimed there were mistakes made by the flight crew, including the crew's inexperience in flying this type of plane, along with poor weather conditions. The crew was said to be preoccupied with other aspects of the flight and failed to monitor the essential flight instruments. This led to new regulations, such as having a flight recorder on all large passenger planes. LaGuardia underwent new construction to extend its runways, improve approach lighting, and even added an instrument landing system.

The crash everyone talks about from this day is not American Airlines Flight 320 but the one referred to as The Day the Music Died. The similarities are spine-chilling. With poor weather, both planes taking off in the Midwest just a few hundred miles apart, instrument readings, and crashing at almost the same miles per hour, among other common factors.

Although coincidental, this is the story of The Winter Dance Party of 1959 that took the lives of Buddy Holly, Ritchie

Valens, the Big Bopper, and pilot Roger Peterson, who had combined record sales in the millions at the time of their deaths. Larry Lehmer wrote in The Day the Music Died in 1997, the overall record sales in 1956 were more than $300 million, which today is roughly 3.5 billion! RCA Victor sold more than 13.5 million Elvis Presley singles.

It's the night the American youth were devastated, some calling it the night the music died.

I refer to it as the night this story began and came alive.

It was one of the saddest days in American rock and roll history and a huge loss to the youth of the fifties. It was the first time that generation lost its innocence, as prior to this, the only major icon loss had been James Dean who was killed in an automobile accident at the age of twenty-four in 1955 in California.

The loss of these rock and roll artists was only the beginning, for many rock stars would die at a young age in the following decades. Though this event in history was so deeply impactful to the zeitgeist of the times, it has been mentioned in numerous songs and films.

Now, please settle in as the following pages take you back to the unmatched era of the late 50s and the artists who left their mark.

An Era of Firsts

"It's the Wolfman! We gonna get down and know each other a bit better. Rock and Roll till Midnight! If you feel like rockin' and rollin', take your shoes off, turn off the lights, and call the law."

~Words spoken from the gravely, growling, raspy voice of the most popular late-night DJ, Wolfman Jack.

If one could find Doc Brown and Marty from Back to the Future and travel back to the 1950s, you would find a time of simplicity that was pure and innocent. When a car pulled up to a gas station, an attendant came to greet you at your window, probably knew your name, asked what type of gasoline you wanted, pumped it, checked your oil, and cleaned your windshield. Yes, a full-service station that was taken for granted. The fifties were a time when one could knock on a stranger's door if in need of help, and they would answer and step into action to help fix a flat tire, pull a car out of the mud, and offer a piece of poundcake on top of it.

Teens were happy and energetic, while the artists' voices were clear and filled with enthusiasm. Lyrics like "Why do birds sing so gay" were sung without a worry that any of the words would be misconstrued.

The Cabaret Tax, which was called "Dance Tax" on the street, was not intended to shut down jazz, swing, and big bands, but it did just that, paving the way to bebop before it was called rock and roll.

The new sound of rock and roll shook America and was a way to communicate in the fifties. It meant something deeply to the younger generation. According to Don Larson, who grew up as a teenager during this time and a Buddy Holly expert, these were simpler days and times. He had fun times at the local ballroom, where he pretty much lived, seeing the likes of Duane Eddy, Buddy Knox, The Fireballs, Jack Scott, Danny and the Juniors, along with Bobby Vee, who he became personal friends with for over thirty-five years.

David Bingham, who was a member of The Roses, would always refer to the fifties singers as being incredibly talented, as they stood out. The songs were personable and about daily life. In those days, there was no such thing as pitch correction or the ability for numerous takes so the best clips can be spliced together to make a track. You see, in the days of yesteryear, the artists had to be perfect all the way through the song or redo the entire thing over again until they got it right.

It was an era where Blacks and Whites played in bands together, even recorded each other's songs and played at the same radio stations. This music helped break down racial barriers between the two genres that had been segregated. Several African American singers and groups did a mix of R&B, country and western, pop, and hillbilly that stemmed from their gospel roots. The term Rock and Roll came to the scene in a frenzy, along with the introduction of a new position called the disc jockey, which was coined by Alan Freed, a DJ himself.

There was the doowop sound that can be heard in the timeless classic "16 Candles" by The Crests. Groups named themselves after birds and insects as they belted tunes about their girlfriends. Bands like The Flamingos, Robins, Larks,

Penguins, and even Crows. They put out songs like "Peggy Sue," sang by Buddy Holly (57); "Donna" by Ritchie Valens (58); "Lucille" by Little Richard (57); "Maybelline" from Gene Vincent (58); "Susie Q" from Dale Hawkins (57); and "Carol," done by Chuck Berry (58). The top songs in the late fifties and early sixties offered such classics as "All Shook Up" by Elvis Presley (1957); "Volare" by Dean Martin (1958); and "Battle of New Orleans" by Johnny Horton (1959).

We saw the rise of car culture with rock and roll music as cars became an important part of people's lives. They were, for once, able to show their individuality, freedom, and at the same time have fun. There was social standing with automobiles, especially if you had a V8 engine in a hot rod! These cars erupted onto the scene in the 50s, some capable of speeds over two hundred miles per hour, with fancy paint jobs and pinstriping. Cars had a radio antenna, and as we entered the space age, they used chrome (and I mean lots of chrome) on large tailfins. The place to be on a Friday or Saturday night in the fifties was Main Street, and by night's end, drag racing occurred, as this became mainstream. Charlie Ryan recorded the hit "Hot Rod Lincoln" about a race, done years later by Commander Cody and His Lost Planet Airmen, which was the more upbeat version and caught on.

Crusin', not cruising, was cool, which was the way teenagers were seen and saw others. Cruisin' to nearby towns looking for someone to race, and of course for the guys to find girls. In California on Van Nuys Blvd, guys had to look good, with their black leather jackets, to fit in with this scene, because you had to be C-O-O-I..

Finding a six-pack of beer was always of importance, sharing with their girl, who rode in the passenger seat.

The introduction of the drive thru or drive-in restaurant started, and carhops were typically girls on roller skates, who would serve the hyped-up teenagers hamburgers and milkshakes to their cars as they waited with the radio on and their girlfriend in tow, chewing their Teaberry Gum that had a strong wintergreen flavor.

The ever-popular A&W and Dog n Suds have been and are still called root beer stands.

The car craze led to a growing number of drive-in theaters across the country that began back in 1933 but saw a boom in the 1950s. Drive-in theaters bring back memories of family time and popcorn—a perfect summer evening while watching a movie together.

Mary Charlson from Clear Lake, IA grew up as a teenager in the fifties, which she described as a fun time where everyone felt safe. Main street, like all other towns, was the place to be, as they would cruise from the A&W drive in on one side of town, honking their horns and waving at others while they headed to Duffy's drive in on the northeast side of town, making a circle all night long. The Hi-Di-Ho drive-in was a major meeting place in the fifties in Lubbock, Texas, which saw the likes of Buddy Holly and The Crickets, where they would later perform as a promotional stunt. It was referred to as "Circling the Ho" by the teenagers, in which they drove around the Hi-Di-Ho.

The Surf Ballroom Wednesday Night Teen Dances were a big thing as well, as each school had its own section. If you had ever been to the Surf, then you would be familiar with the small, dark green booths still in use today that Mary and six to eight of her friends would cram into as young teenagers.

A place that sticks out to me each time I drive from Las Vegas to Los Angeles is Peggy Sue's Diner in Yermo, CA, boasting a backdrop of the Calico Mountains, ten miles north of Barstow, CA at basically the halfway point of the trip. Picture a 50s jukebox of King Kong-size at the entrance to the diner, where the old songs still play. It opened in 1954 with just nine counter stools and three booths. Today it features a 5 and Dime store, pizza parlor, old fashioned ice cream malts, sundaes, and Rockin' Robin Floats. The menu is full of drinks, burgers, specials, and sandwiches named after popular fifties stars, and all three artists from this story are included.

To start the day off, the breakfast menu at Peggy Sue's features the Oh Boy! omelet, with lunch offering choices of the Peggy Sue Special, which is a 50s style cheeseburger, Buddy Holly bacon cheeseburger, the La Bamba Burger that is a 50s style chili burger, Big Bopper BLT, and even Ritchie Valens fries. A definite throwback to the days of traveling in a car with your parents as a child. Oh, and on the way out, it's See You Later Alligator, which was a hit by Bill Haley and His Comets!

Groups played on local radio stations for exposure and notoriety, while teenagers would sit in their bedroom with their new device called the transistor radio. It was a time when music on the radio selected by DJs made them feel like adults.

Nelson Crabb, the mayor of Clear Lake, Iowa, reminisced growing up in Franklin, NJ, a zinc mining town at the time, with his 1930 Model A Ford that didn't have a radio. He went to the junkyard to get one so he could listen to the songs of that era, sporting a crew cut. In high school, they weren't allowed to wear jeans, only khaki pants, and at noon they would go out to the parking lot to turn on the radio while his friends snuck a smoke before heading back to class.

After crusin', hitting the drive-in for a shake and a burger while listening to the popular music on the radio, there was only one thing to do. Go to the school dance—a SOCK HOP! These hit the scene around 1944 and became a teenage fad in 1948, usually held at high schools in the gymnasium or cafeterias. The term was coined because it was required to remove hard-soled shoes to protect the varnished floor. These sock hops are strongly associated with the 1950s and the start of rock 'n roll. "At the Hop" by Danny and the Juniors hit the airwaves in 1957 and was instantly a hit, with lyrics about popular dances you would see at a sock hop such as the bunny hop, stroll, and limbo rock.

Teenage girls thought guys were "dreamy" and hoped to go steady with them. Guys referred to girls as "babes" and everything was bitchin'. Terms like "golly gee" and "whoops a daisy" were commonly used, and John Wonsmos once commented that his group used the phrase "that'll be the day" all the time.

The first teenage fashion trend of the 50s was poodle skirts, which were a solid color, wide swing, felt skirt with a design of a coiffed poodle, flamingo, flowers, and even hot rod cars on them. Girls had found a way to show their personalities. These skirts went to the knee or just below, and when they spun on the dance floor, the skirt would flare out, which made them great for sock hops.

The guys, or "greasers" as they were known, developed their own fashion style by rolling their cigarette packs in their sleeve. This was made popular by James Dean in the movies and later by Fonzie in the television show, Happy Days. The guys were considered "cool," with their slicked-back hairstyle and t-shirts with their cigs rolled up because the tight jeans of that era would crush them. Smoking was socially acceptable during this time and was even fashionable.

Don McLean stated, "The 50s started around 1956-1957. Prior to that, everything was black and white. To us, all that music was important, and to have it all taken away abruptly at such a young age was a terrible shock." (Buddy Holly-Rave On: The Story of Buddy Holly, 2017)

The loss of three rock and roll stars was felt deeply, as shown in the 1973 classic film American Graffiti, where the character John, played by Paul Le Mat, was a cool teen riding around town in a muscle car with a young McKenzie Phillips, who played Carol. In the film, John turns off the radio as a Beach Boys surfing tune is playing and says, "Rock and Roll has been going downhill ever since Buddy Holly died." Buddy Holly had poignantly expressed the feelings of this generation through his music.

The soundtrack for the film features an image of a girl from a drive-in wearing a Mel's Diner hat and holding a plate of food with a filled root beer, featuring hits from the 50s that include Buddy Holly's "Maybe Baby" and "That'll Be the Day" along with The Big Bopper's "Chantilly Lace." If you listen closely, you'll hear the click of the needle moving over as the vinyl 45 record hits the plastic turntable and starts to spin. The needle finds the groove on the record, the cracking sound of the way music was meant to be heard begins, and then…. That oh so distinctive sound of the fifties begins! Dilla

(Niederfrank) Arneson who lived in Garner, IA at the time summed up the 50s perfectly: "I'd love to live it again!"

Jiles Perry (JP) Richardson *AKA*
The Big Bopper (28)

Born October 24, 1930 to Jiles Perry Sr., who was an oil field worker/driller, and Elsie Richardson.

"Jape," as friends called him, was a quiet and thoughtful person, whereas his alter ego, The Big Bopper, was flamboyant, loud, with lots of charisma and a huge personality.

Jerry Boynton, who recently passed away, was a close friend and co-worker to JP at KTRM. He was interviewed by Anthony Garcia in March of 2024, and you can watch it in its entirety https://www.youtube.com/@nthonymusic. Boynton stated that Richardson was a funny guy who was a terrific storyteller. In a letter written to JP Jr. from Dick Clark in 1988, he told how he remembered that JP disliked his real name and that JP sounded better. It's ironic that today he's hardly known as JP but as The Big Bopper.

JP wore #85 as a defensive lineman on the "Royal Purple" football team at Beaumont High School and had the nickname "killer." He graduated in 1947 and entered pre-law studies at Lamar College. While in college, he worked part-time at KTRM, which is now KZZB. By 1949, he had quit college and was hired full-time at a radio station, where he eventually was promoted to supervisor of announcers.

JP was drafted to the US Army in March of 1955. He served two years as a radar instructor at Fort Bliss, which is close to El Paso, Texas. Richardson was discharged with the rank of Corporal in March of 1957.

Returning to KTRM, he worked the eleven a.m. to twelvethirty p.m. shift Monday through Friday, then moved to three to six p.m. and became the program director. He broke the record for continuous on-air broadcasting, with a remote setup from the lobby of Jefferson Theatre in downtown Beaumont, referred to as "Jape-a-thon" and totaled five days, two hours, and eight minutes, where he played 1,821 records. He showered during the five-minute newscasts.

Richardson wasn't done after the Jape-a-thon and eventually became known for doing crazy things, such as rolling eggs in downtown Beaumont at Easter, racing Slim Watts from Beaumont to a nearby town riding lawn mowers, and even racing a man while he drove a car and his competitor went down the Neches River in a motorboat.

The Big Bopper even today is said to be a one-hit wonder, but he was much more than that. He is credited with the term "music video" in 1959 when he recorded himself.

Disc Magazine, which was the Billboard magazine of England at the time, released an issue ten days before he died, featuring a subtitle "The Big Bopper blazes a trail that could revolutionize the disc biz." He made predictions that records would be filmed! Songs would be released on a video tape. He mentioned that you would have to be good not just vocally but visually and explained about a device you would hook up to your television to record. This would become the VCR or videocassette recorder, which was a device where you could record and played back television programs or movies on magnetic tape cassettes. He had an idea for a video jukebox and was decades ahead of MTV!

Boynton explained that his first release on Mercury was called "Beggar to a King" by Jape and the Japetts. The song went nowhere but is a beautiful ballad. He was a prolific songwriter, as this was his aspiration in addition to buying a radio station. He wrote fifty-five songs in total. JP developed the afternoon three p.m. segment called the "Eh Show," where he would have conversations with a rubber frog named Aloysius, a character born by squeezing air out of the frog into his own mouth, and he created an illusion that he and Aloysius were having a conversation, which resulted in nothing but laughter.

Inspired by the memories of the Sabine River, where he heard Indian tribe stories, he wrote the song "Running Bear" for his friend Johnny Preston. JP sang background on the track, and it was released after his death, where it rose to #1 on the charts.

Harold "Pappy" Daily signed JP to Mercury Records, where he recorded "Chantilly Lace" as The Big Bopper on Daily's D Label, which climbed to the top of the charts in the summer of 1958 and stayed in the Top 40 for twenty-two weeks. It earned him a gold record after being listed among the Top 100 for twenty-five weeks. "Chantilly Lace," according to Lehmer at one point, was the third most played record in the nation and was released in thirty-seven total countries.

In 1958, Jerry, who was his engineer, went to pick up JP to take him to Houston to record the song, "The Purple People Eater Meets the Witch Doctor," as Richardson's wife was out of the town at the time. On the ride to Houston, Boynton asked him what song he was going to record for the "B" side of the record. JP said he wasn't sure but had a couple of ideas, one of which was "Chantilly Lace," and explained he would have a phone conversation with a chick. He ended up doing eighteen takes to record the song and each one was different than the other because Big Bopper was a master ad-libber and would just say whatever came to his mind. He was killed before he saw any of the profits from "Chantilly Lace." The single earned a gold record, which he was set to receive on February 8th.

Linwood Sasser, who is "The Big Bopper" in John Mueller's Winter Dance Party Tribute Show, explained that he imagines what JP may have done on stage performing "Chantilly Lace" from watching what videos are out there of him to study his moves and adds his own dynamic action to it while placing himself in his shoes.

The Big Bopper got his name after seeing several college students doing a dance at the time called "the bop" and decided to call himself the Big Bopper. JP played guitar, and when he heard the songs "Purple People Eater" by Sheb Wooley and "Witch Doctor" by Ross Bagdasarian performed under his stage name of David Seville, he put them together and recorded "The Purple People Eater Meets The Witch Doctor." The B side to this record was "Chantilly Lace." His song "White Lightning" became George Jones's first number one hit in 1959.

At the time of the plane crash, JP's savings account showed a balance of just $8.00. His assets included a Dodge Sedan valued at $400 and guitar that was worth $100. He was building a recording studio at his home in Beaumont, Texas and was planning on investing in a radio station.

JP was married to Adrianne Joyce "Teetsie" Fryou, who passed away in 2004. They had a daughter Debra, who passed in 2006 and a son JP Richardson Jr., who died in 2013. He

23

was born just months after the crash that took his father's life. Richardson, according to Boynton, was working to take care of his family. Boynton did have one personal item that was in his coat pocket when his body was found—a pack of Chesterfield cigarettes, as JP was a heavy smoker.

JP was thrown approximately forty feet into the field beyond where the plane came to rest. He was wearing a red-checkered flannel shirt and light blue cotton pants with no jacket.

According to the autopsy report, his personal effects included: a gold wedding ring, one small gold flat key, a pair of dice, a guitar pick, a black billfold containing numerous cards, receipts, a Texas driver's license, musicians' ID cards, and $272.53 in cash.

Something that is of note that may be surprising is that $11.65 was taken from the deceased for the coroner's fees. The coroner's fees breakdown was $10 for the inquest or investigation, .65 for mileage at .07 per mile, and one dollar for the docket case.

The funeral was held on Friday, February 6th in Beaumont, TX. Elvis sent yellow roses. The Big Bopper is buried in Beaumont, Texas at Forest Lawn Cemetery.

Dion DiMucci said, "The Bopper could light up a room. He was a fun-loving guy."

There was a conspiracy regarding his death. Two months after the crash, an Iowa farmer found a 22-caliber pistol that had belonged to Buddy Holly. In 2007, JP Richardson Jr. called Dr. Bill Bass, who was a rock star in the field of forensic anthropology. Richardson wondered if his father had survived the crash and whether he was going for help or was he shot? The body of The Big Bopper was exhumed and was in remarkable condition. JP Jr. was there when the casket was opened. Bass stated the casket was difficult to open. His father was wearing a black suit with a blue and gray striped tie. His thick brown hair was still in his familiar 50s flat-top. JP Jr. had never met his father because he was born just months after the crash. Try to imagine the moment—the first time you see your parent is when they bring them up from the grave…

JP Jr. sat with his father for an hour and a half, communicating silently.

An x-ray autopsy was conducted from the top of the skull to the bottom of the feet. The Big Bopper was broken from top to bottom with over two hundred fractures, which included massive skull fractures. Dr. Bass concluded there was no way he could have survived, and he found no indication of any gunshot wounds He concluded he died immediately, and the conspiracy was put to rest. He was placed in a new casket when reburied, and the first casket is on display at the Roadside America Museum in Hillsboro, TX.

Albert Juhl the farmer who found the gun told Sheriff Allen the gun still worked because he fired into the air which accounted for the only missing cartridge from the firearm. He fired the only shot not anyone else.

A briefcase he had with him was loaned to the Surf Ballroom by JP Jr. The briefcase had survived the crash, bearing his initials on the front, and contains a notebook that is filled with songs he was working on. In addition, it holds another notebook filled with songs The Big Bopper wrote as a boy, and a hotel receipt for $3.75 from February 1st, 1959 from Ironwood, MI was donated.

Bopper was inducted into the Rockabilly Hall of Fame in 1997, Texas Country Hall of Fame in 2004, and Texas Radio Hall of Fame in 2008. Jay Jr., aka Big Bopper Jr., performed all around the globe with The Winter Dance Party Tribute Show, and on some of the very same stages that his father once did.

Charles Hardin Holley *AKA*
Buddy Holly (22)

Born on September 7th, 1936 to Lawrence and Ella Holley.

At age five, he won five dollars singing "Did You Ever Go Sailing (Down the River of Memories)." He was an outdoorsman who loved to fish, play baseball, draw (especially horses), do woodworking, art, and leatherworking. He liked to get away from it all and even hunt rabbits.

The Holleys were a humble family, and Buddy was shy and quiet off stage, changing into a different person on stage and, as they say, cut loose!

Sherry Holley, Buddy's niece, saw him a lot, and they went on fishing trips together. She recalls a camping trip like it was yesterday to Creede, CO, where she and her mom slept on top of the car.

Buddy met Bob Montgomery in 1951 in the 7th grade at Hutchinson Jr. High School, and the two became Buddy and Bob. They were managed by Hipockets Duncan, who was a radio disc jockey at KDAV, where they played requests for the KDAV Sunday Party. The station is now KRFE AM 580, "The Station That Listens to Lubbock." They also played at the Lawson Roller Rink, which is a Lubbock Historic Landmark that was constructed in 1950 and in the fall of '56 was the American Legion Youth Center on weekends, where Holly signed a one-year contract to be the house band. They played grocery store parking lots, on the roof of the Womble Oldsmobile car dealership, and even the Cotton Club.

Buddy attended Lubbock High School in Texas, which now has a small exhibit in its main hallway, and he made his first appearance on local television in 1952. In 1955, after seeing Elvis Presley, he decided to pursue a career in music. He is regarded by some as the artist who defined traditional rock and roll with the lineup of two guitars, bass, and drums.

In high school, Buddy played in a country-style band, which transitioned into adding a third member to the duo. Larry Welborn played bass and joined them on October 14th, 1955, which changed their names to Buddy, Bob, and Larry. The trio performed at the Sunday Party, which was held at Fair Park Auditorium. The show's promoter, Eddie Crandall, was so impressed with Holly, he told him that he would try to get them a recording contract. Decca Records offered only Buddy a contract in January of 1956. The first recording session was held in Nashville on January 26th, 1956, with Buddy, Don Guess, and Sonny Curtis at the Owen Bradley Studio. The record "That'll Be the Day" went nowhere, as it was originally a country and western song! After they recorded, "That'll Be the Day" Bradley remarked it was the worst song he ever heard.

Holly's hit "Peggy Sue" was originally written as "Cindy Lou" after Buddy's niece. The title was changed to Peggy Sue in reference to Peggy Sue Gerron, who passed away in 2018. Gerron was the girlfriend and future wife of drummer Jerry Allison, and he had a crush on her. They had temporarily broken up when the song was recorded. Gerron stated the first time she heard the song was at the Sacramento Memorial Auditorium in 1958 as Buddy Holly and the Crickets were performing it. She had been shocked, as it was a total surprise. She had been invited to the show by Jerry's mother, who then got permission from Peggy's mother. She had no idea the song was written or recorded. The band started the show with "That'll Be Day" and went straight into "Peggy Sue."

In 2008, Buddy Holly's widow Maria Elena Holly went to court to prevent Peggy Sue from selling a 283-page book she wrote regarding her friendship with Holly. According to Maria, Buddy did not consider Peggy Sue a friend. Gerron claimed that all the stories she wrote were taken from her diary and Buddy was one of her best friends.

In 1956, Decca label released his single "Blue Days Black Nights" which went nowhere, though it's a really good song. Buddy Holly and The Crickets recorded a rock version of "That'll Be the Day" on February 25th, 1957, which Decca released accidentally without any rights in June of that year. The song had been written in about thirty minutes by drummer Jerry Allison. The record stated it was sung by The Crickets, and by September, it was one of the best-selling records in rock and roll as well as rhythm and blues.

1958 saw Holly either as a solo artist or with The Crickets, and he cut a hit record every other month! The Crickets were the first white act booked sight unseen at the Apollo Theatre on August 16th, 1957. The audience booed them a little at first, but by the end of their third night there, they had won over the crowd with their energy and music.

Sherry is the daughter of Larry Holley and was only seven years old at the time of Uncle Buddy's death. She vividly remembers him just as Uncle Buddy but recalls the time she realized Uncle Buddy was a rock and roll star, as her parents made the decision to stay home from church on a Sunday evening, which was something she stated they never did! This was to watch Buddy perform on the Ed Sullivan Show, which was his debut.

Sherry put her head down and said, "I do remember the last song Buddy sang at our house, it was "Raining in My Heart" in my dad's living room. He almost made my dad cry, as he said it was the most beautiful song he ever heard. She then added, "It was the last time he was ever at our house."

Sherry herself started writing songs around the age of thirteen and loves to perform. Her favorite song of Uncle Buddy's to perform is one he didn't write, "Send Me Some Lovin'," and opens her show with the first big hit, "That'll Be the Day." She expressed that it is phenomenal music that grabs you. "It's happy music. People can relate to it and kids like it."

The 1955 Fender Stratocaster is referred to as the Holy Grail of rock and roll. His first two Fender Stratocaster guitars were stolen while on tour. The first was a 1954 model that was taken in 1957 at a tour stop in Detroit, MI. He then bought a 1957 model that was stolen in St. Louis, MO. The Fender he used at the 1959 Winter Dance Party was a 1958 model and is now on display at the Buddy Holly Center. To this day, the whereabouts of the two stolen guitars are unknown. Tommy Townsend, a country artist who was mentored by Waylon Jennings, informed me that at one time, Jerry Bridges, a Hall of Fame musician, had Buddy's Fender Tweed amp, which was really worn! Tommy played through the amp, which he said had a great sound and felt was a deluxe reverb model, has since been sold to a collector.

Sherry felt Buddy could do it all and was always busy singing and producing. Before New York, Holly created his own record company called Prism Records and added a publishing company titled Taupe. He had bought the land where he was going to build a recording studio. From a business card that was already printed, Buddy was the president, Norman Petty was listed as sales and Ron Rush as promotions. The address on the card was 1221 W. Seventh St., Clovis, NM, which was right by the Norman Petty Studio. The plans were made, as he had visions of adding a house, into which he was going to move his parents. Buddy's parents gave tours of their home on 56th street, where they moved after his death, and even allowed a few individuals to play his acoustic guitar! Sherry herself even slept on Uncle Buddy's bed that is on display at the Buddy Holly Center. The Holley family moved all over the Lubbock area. The last house he lived in was 1606 39th St. in 1958. He was born at the family home, which is no longer there, located at 1911 6th St.

The name The Crickets was due to Buddy being fond of a band called The Spiders. He passed on names such as Grasshoppers and even The Beatles, as Buddy thought that name was a little corny. The group, Buddy Holly and Crickets played together from 1956 to 1958, as they split in December of '58 over a difference between Buddy's ambition and musical taste, as Holly was a headstrong person. Waylon Jennings took over as bassist, and Tommy Allsup took over guitar, while Carl Bunch replaced Jerry Allison on the drums. The other two original members of The Crickets were Nikki Sullivan and Joe Mauldin.

Buddy may have been the first rock and roll artist to be involved in every aspect of his music, which included arranging and record production. He played rock and roll for just two short years but made an impact that is still felt to this day in popular music. From August of 1957 to August of 1958, Buddy and The Crickets saw seven Top 40 songs hit the charts. He was inducted into the Rock and Roll Hall of Fame in 1986.

On October 21st, 1958, the final recording session of Holly's is known as The String Sessions, as he recorded four songs in three and a half hours at the Pythian Temple on West 70th Street in New York City which featured an eighteen-piece ensemble, directed by Dick Jacobs. Those four songs are "True Love Ways" (which Vi Petty recorded first but was not released), "Moondreams," "Raining In My Heart," and "It Doesn't Matter Anymore."

Paul Anka and Buddy Holly were friends, and Anka wrote the song "It Doesn't Matter Anymore" specifically for Holly, who recorded it in 1958. This track became Holly's last single.

These are the best four songs Buddy Holly ever recorded in my opinion. "True Love Ways" was Buddy's song for Maria. Holly wrote thirty songs and recorded nine Top 10 records in just eighteen months, and many have been covered and remade by numerous other artists. As Don Larson put it, Buddy Holly was an underdog and did not get the credit he deserved when he was alive. Larson simply said, "He was a genius! There is no other way around it."

Buddy Holly was known for many hits. Some of his more popular include "That'll Be the Day," "Peggy Sue," and "Oh Boy." Sonny West wrote "Oh Boy" but called it "All My Love." David Bingham and The Roses were backup singers on tracks 'It's So Easy" and "Think It Over."

He was a visionary artist ahead of his time and gone too soon. He was the first musician to take control of his music, which at that time was groundbreaking, with a unique sound all to himself.

The correct spelling of the family name is Holley. It was changed to Holly after Decca Records wrote Holly on the contract, which Buddy just let it go, and it stuck.

Holly's career wasn't doing good amidst financial troubles, so he agreed to go on the Winter Dance Party Tour of 1959. There are several writings and some people who blame Norman Petty for Buddy's financial problems. Sources state that there are documents from late 1957 and 1958 showing Buddy was paid in advance of the breakup between Norman and Buddy. From the outside looking in, it does seem Buddy had a taste for the finer things in life, as he purchased a 1958 Ariel Cyclone Limited Edition Motorcycle, which was one of only two hundred made. He bought it from Ray Miller's Motorcycle Shop in Dallas, TX at the same time Jerry Allison bought a Triumph Trophy. In addition to the bikes, they bought Levi jackets and peaked hats adorned with wings, riding them home in a thunderstorm 350 miles. He purchased top of the line guitars, clothes, and a bedroom set. Could he have overspent the money he was given? Even if he did, it does not diminish his long-lasting legacy, as so many rock and rollers have spent all the money they made.

At the Norman Petty Studio in Clovis, NM, they were creative to get different sounds, such as running different lengths of ceramic drainage tile to create an echo chamber that was located next door above his father's garage. According to Bingham, the climate controlled space had a crisper sound at night. Take a listen to the song, "I'm Gonna Love You Too," and at the very end, listen closely for crickets that were in the

Norman Petty studio. They deemed it bad luck to kill them and left them in the recording.

When they were getting ready to record the song, "Everyday" at the Norman Petty Studio, Jerry Allison was out in the lobby practicing the drums by slapping his hands and knees. Petty heard him doing it, put a microphone on it, and had him do this on the recording instead of using the drums. When the song starts, you can clearly hear Allison playing the beat off knees and hands. On the track, "Not Fade Away" he was playing a cardboard box in lieu of the drums. Petty and Holly were imaginative in creating different sounds that stood out. Holly was among the first to use techniques known as doubletracking in the studio.

As an interesting note, The Rolling Stones' first U.S. release was a cover of Holly's "Not Fade Away."

Norman Petty
Norman Petty Studio

Norman Petty was from Clovis, NM, where in high school, he did a regular fifteen-minute radio show and later in life would own a radio station. He was thirteen years old when he started making records at his father's gas station and then later converted a family grocery store into the Norman Petty Studio, which included his wife Vi and Jack Vaughn. They put together The Norman Petty Trio.

Jack Vaughn was the guitarist, and his wife was a vocalist. The trio was named Most Promising Instrumental Group in 1954 by Cashbox Magazine and landed a record deal with RCA after the release of "Mood Indigo," which sold five hundred thousand copies.

Norman won his first writers award in 1957 for their track "Almost Paradise," which charted as high as #18. As one of the founding fathers of early rock and roll and a creative producer, Norman started his publishing company Nor-Va-Jak Music (Nor from Norman, VA from Violet Ann, and Jak from Jack Vaughn.) The Norman Petty Studio owns approximately two thousand copyrights to music that nobody has ever heard!

He became a record producer once he built his own state-of the-art studio, which opened in 1957 on 7th street in Clovis. Norman charged by the session instead of by the hour, which was $75 per side of a recording. The studio saw the likes of Roy Orbison, Waylon Jennings, and Buddy Knox. It was billed as the "go-to" studio in the early 60s.

David Bingham (The Roses) became a session vocalist for Petty to fill voids in recordings. To this day, it is referred to as an authentic vintage studio, preserving how it had been in the fifties. He produced most Buddy Holly's records between 1956-58 mainly at his Clovis Studio, but there were some recorded at Ball Sound Studios in New York. In an interview on May 29th, 2024, Jim Liddane for the International Songwriters Association said, "My first impression of him (Holly) was of a person ultra-eager to succeed. He wore a Tshirt and Levis. Really, he was unimpressive to look at but impressive to hear. In fact, businessmen around here asked me why I was interested in a hillbilly like Holly, and I told them I thought Buddy was a diamond in the rough."

Petty became the band's manager at the request of Buddy and took control of the money, along with their career. He later was allegedly accused of holding royalty payments and Holly became aware that these deposits had been put into Petty's bank and not The Crickets', which eventually resulted in their parting ways. Records show that Norman always did the best he could to make sure Buddy and the Crickets had what was owed and what was needed, resulting in a complex circumstances. The broken ties between Holly and Petty caused friction. Norman needed to look at the books to see what was owed to Holly, which at the same time was when Southern Music (publisher) and Decca Records stopped making payment to the Norman Petty Studio. Money stopped coming in, as everyone was auditing their books. Petty sent telegrams for over four years to Decca asking for his money, which were all ignored. To complicate the matter more, The Crickets stayed on with Petty. According to sources close to the Petty story, there are ledger books at the Norman Petty Studio that show in 1957 and 1958, money was being paid to

Buddy Holly, one entry in '58 for $60,000. Petty has been accused of everything from withholding royalties, being a racist, along with his wife, and even for the cause of Holly's death. He did not once defend his actions in interviews that are in print or video. Norman only had positive things to say about Buddy Holly despite all the accusations. My feeling is Petty felt he knew the truth and kept those matters private, which has allowed people to come to their own conclusions about what did or did not happen.

Petty also added his name to songwriting credits, and from what I have been told, for the most part, the songs that Norman added his name to were ones he had a big part in writing. The obvious exception is "That'll Be the Day," which was written by Buddy and Jerry before they went to Clovis, but a business decision was made to add Norman's name for the best interest of both parties. In this time period, this was common practice, as managers, producers, and record company owners would often be given songwriting credits in return for the work in promoting a record. Many understood this was done and agreed to the terms.

Norman Petty was part of numerous hit records, from "That'll Be the Day" to "Sugar Shack" by The Fireballs. In 1964, the accounting books showed that "Sugar Shack" made over $100,000 in three of the four quarters that year. Holly's songs, "Rave On" and "It's So Easy" saw disappointing sales.

Payola was a huge ordeal in the late 50s, which was the illegal practice of paying a radio station or disc jockey to play and promote a song without disclosing these payments. Disc Jockey Alan Freed (NY) and Stan Richard (Boston), along with record companies, bribed record companies to ensure certain songs or artists received airtime. The Association of

Society of Composing and Publishers (ASCAP) and Broadcast Music Incorporated (BMI) were involved. Norman Petty was strongly against Payola and would not pay, thus many of Holly's songs did not chart as they should have but are classic hits today. The irony of this is these same songs were charting in England where there was no Payola. In addition to this scandal, the selling of counterfeit records was prevalent, which made it difficult to account for actual sales of records. "Many in the 1950s record business were mobsters, racketeers, and money launderers. They were middlemen between the retailer and Clovis. Norman, who was an independent small businessman, was often dealing with professional crooks with known mob ties and was at their mercy in the same way as the exploited artists." (The King of Clovis, Frank Blanas, 2014).

Buddy wanted to become a bigger name, whereas his wife Maria felt Norman wasn't fit to be his manager. In November 1958, a blowup occurred with Maria Elena, Vi, Norman Petty, and Buddy Holly. Even when Buddy asked to end the financial/manager partnership, he wanted to know if Petty could still record him. Norman quipped. "Over my dead body!" Things were obviously said in the heat of the moment when friction and strain were at an all-time high. These raw emotions were amplified, and unfortunately they stayed that way due to Holly's death.

Petty later felt that the reason for the split was because he didn't do a competent job of promoting Buddy as an artist. Before 1956-57, Buddy was an unknown artist, and by 1959, he was known worldwide, which came from the songs produced by Petty.

From all my research, it is my conclusion that Maria Elena was the main cause for the split between Holly and Petty, as she wanted the couple to have more control over their finances, and on top of that she did not have a good relationship with Norman. Maria Elena worked at PeerSouthern Music, which was the company that handled Norman Petty's publishing business. It had been said that Buddy told Maria as they were walking out of the studio after a dispute to wait a minute, "These are my friends."

Norman's career after Buddy surpassed the earning he made with Holly, mainly due to writing the song, "Wheels," which The String-A-Longs recorded in 1960. After Holly's death, at the request of the family, Norman finished the overdubbing of the unfinished recordings and demos that ended up charting overseas.

Sherry Holley looked forward to trips to Clovis after Buddy died, as the family had business to deal with. In 1999, a lawsuit was brought on by the Norman Petty Estate and the Holley family. The estate fought hard, along with Maria Elena, to make sure that all parties received their full royalties. They worked together to fight MCA on this and eventually won. MCA owed the Petty Estate and the Holly Heirs a combined amount of $251,325.

Norman closed the studio in 1969 and passed away on August 15th, 1984 after battling leukemia. Vi had the studio restored in 1982 after a fire damaged the echo chamber, which was located next door at Nor-Va-Jak Music. She reopened the Norman Petty Studio for tours on September 7th, 1986, which was Buddy Holly's fiftieth birthday.

Kenneth Broad picked up the pieces after Norman passed away. After Norman died, Kenneth was faced with saving the estate, putting the publishing back in order, and turning the studio profitable again. He was instrumental in helping Vi move forward and was involved in several legal battles with record labels and publishers. Without Kenneth, there would be no studio, and all its history would be lost.

The Contract

I took a photo of a framed contract in the studio that was an interesting find. It states that Nor Va Jak Music was the publisher, and Buddy Holly was the composer. The first eyeopening thought was that there are many who state there was no contract between Holly and Petty, and Buddy was free to leave anytime he wanted to. This contract was written on September 12th, 1958, for a period of five years (September 12th, 1963). Here are some of the key components.

The composer will write music and lyrics exclusively for the publisher. Agrees to sell, assign, transfer to the publisher ALL rights whatsoever including public performances for the entire work, conveys an irrevocable power of attorney empowering the publisher to file application and renew copyrights in the name of the composer.

The publisher will make reasonable efforts to publish and exploit the music of the composer.

The publisher agrees to pay royalties as follows: .03 cents of each regular piano or orchestration printed and sold by publisher in United States of America. 50% of net received by publisher for mechanical royalties, synchronizing fees, transcription fees, foreign royalties, and performance fees. Payable on a fixed and determined basis.

In the event that a composition has not been wholly written by composer, the above royalties shall be paid jointly and in equal shares to all writers and if lyrics are written for a composer other than in original language, the publisher shall have the right to deduct from royalties the cost but no more than half.

Statements shall be rendered on February 15th and August 15th of each year. It is agreed "publisher" has option and right to renew and extend agreement for same terms for an additional period of 5 years by written notice through registered mail to the composer no later than 30 days prior to end of agreement.

The contract also stated they would be using the laws of the state of New York. It was witnessed by Norma Jean Berry and Bob Montgomery and signed by Buddy Holly and Norman Petty.

Visiting the studio located in Clovis, NM, you are instantly spun back to a different time. The lobby is full of hit 45 framed records, with furniture to match the era of the fifties, and many records that are "Sample not for Sale" promos. The Crickets drummer J.I. Allison set up in the lobby during recordings.

For those who are into music history or have been in the industry, your first step into the control room will overload your senses in what to take first. Kenneth Broad, the tour guide, does an excellent job of explaining what took place. The Altec speakers in the control room are the originals, which are suspended, as Norman was forward-thinking to avoid any vibrations from solid surfaces. They are vacuum tube-powered and have never been reconned! They put out a deep, crisp sound that you can literally feel, especially coming from a recording that was dubbed from the original master tapes. The studio is filled with several precious time-period microphones, and you can almost hear those who used them talking and singing into them.

You see, the radio in the fifties is what moved songs up the charts. Petty recorded music at night, as the studio at that time was located on a highway and there was less noise in the evening. In those days, they could write and record a song in about four hours' time, as was the case with "Peggy Sue," as Broad played a clip of Petty explaining this song started at around five-thirty a.m. one morning and was finished around nine-thirty a.m.

Randy Brown, who accompanied me on my trip to Clovis and Lubbock, captured what he called "Tommy's Moment." Broad was sitting behind the control board and told me to stay close by, as he was going to play The Crickets' first big hit. He explained that in those days, they wanted to know what it would sound like on the radio, and Norman would let them in at his request to hear the playback. He then told me to sit down in the chair next to where he was sitting. As I was in the process of sitting down, he tells me, "In this chair, where Buddy Holly sat, it's the same chair he sat in to listen to the playback."

He played "That'll Be the Day," and my body felt numb as my face lit up in disbelief that I was sitting in the exact chair and spot as Holly, hearing the master tape playback of the first big hit.

The rest of the tour consists of entering the recording studio with several original pieces from the days of Holly and The Crickets, and the apartment in the back that seems like they were just there and have stepped out for a bit but will be back any moment. Those who grew up in the 50s or 60s will recognize the furniture, kitchen appliances, as well as the tile and décor. It is simply magnificent!

Here is a transcript from an interview from Roy Orbison with Red Robinson who was a legendary Vancouver DJ. He tells us about his first meeting with Buddy Holly in Lubbock, Texas. Orbison recorded his hit "Ooby Dooby" at the Petty Studio after being turned down by Sam Phillips at Sun Records in 1956. After hearing the song, Phillips then asked Orbison how fast he could get there.

Orbison: "Buddy and the Crickets came backstage and said hello and introduced themselves to me. They were a local group, and then shortly thereafter, I heard a record on some station in West Texas by Buddy Holly. It was his first record "Blue Days Black Nights" and the first record that I know of that he recorded. Then he came to Odessa (TX) and we were about ninety miles apart from Odessa, a hundred and twenty from Wink, Texas, and so I went to his show. It was out at the football stadium, and I called him down to the fence and we said hello. I told him I enjoyed the show, so then we kept in touch in a roundabout way."

Robinson: "And your careers both rose."

Orbison: "Yeah, I was first, and then he had to come see my show, and then I went to see his, and then pretty soon, he went out of sight with the songs "Peggy Sue" and "That'll Be the Day.""

Here is Red Robison with Jerry Allison as he talks about the early days with Holly.

Allison: "Buddy started out playing with a fella named Bob Montgomery. They grew up together in grade school and junior high. They just did strictly country music and really hillbilly music, actually wouldn't call it country. They had a country group together when I first started playing in the group, and they had a steel guitar, a stand-up bass, and Sonny Curtis played the fiddle in that band. This was back in 1954-55 and we'd play at service station openings and any place there was to play and played a few joints, but we were really too young to get into them."

Robinson: "Were you kids in high school at the time?"

Allison: "Yeah, we were still in high school when we started doing all that. We play on weekends, you know, out of town maybe a hundred miles, but I must have been a junior in high school when we started, and Buddy and Sonny was a year ahead of me, and so they graduated. They started doing more gigs when they got out of high school of course."

Robinson: "Then you started touring, and at one point, I understand, that Elvis Presley either played at Lubbock or somewhere close. Were you featured on that bill with Presley at that time?"

Allison: "Well, there was a guy named Dave Stone that owned the KDAV radio station then, and we hung around the radio station, so we got backstage to all the shows, and they let us, like, open the show when Elvis came one time, and Buddy used Elvis's guitar and broke a string and did one of Elvis's songs, which was pretty crazy. I mean, Elvis wasn't on RCA yet, he was still on Sun Records, and he was sort of like one of the guys, but I mean he was hot. You know, I mean, he tore it up on the shows, but we weren't on the bill, we just hopped on the show, and nobody knew we were going to, but we started to talk to somebody to let us do it, you know."

Robinson: "What happened, though? I mean, did you start doing rock and roll? At what point did you abandon country?"

Allison: "We did play country shows, and Buddy got more playing rock and roll. In fact, we went to Wichita Falls, Texas one time and cut some demos to try to get a record deal with Bob off the country band, and then we cut some demos. At that time, without Bob, it was just an Elvis type group because we'd already gotten one because we'd been doing Elvis's kind of shows. In fact, I was out of the group for a while because Elvis didn't have a drummer, and so Buddy just had Sonny Curtis playing guitar and Don Guess playing bass. The next time Elvis came through, he had a drummer, and I was back in the group."

Robinson: "That's when DJ Fontana joined the Presley group. DJ came through there with Scotty (Moore) and Bill (Black) and Elvis at one point, that's what you're saying…"

Allison: "When he first started coming through, we cut some records and some like a country-type record, and then Buddy cut some, but Bob Montgomery didn't like rock and roll at all. I think we cut a couple of Elvis ones, some written like trying to copy Elvis's type of writing. We cut those, and they wanted to sign that group, they wanted to sign Buddy Holly but not the country stuff, and so then we said, 'Okay,' and the country deal went down the tubes."

Robinson: "That's when it became rock and roll for The Crickets. Was "That'll Be the Day" really from the John Wayne movie The Searchers?"

Allison: "We'd already cut "That'll Be the Day" for Decca, and you know the deal, where you can't cut the same song for different record companies, and so we just called it The

46

Crickets instead of Buddy Holly and The Crickets. Oh yeah, Buddy had seen that movie either the night before or two before we wrote that, and John Wayne said that a lot in that movie, but, yeah, that's definitely where that came from."

Robinson: "I think with the legend of anybody, whether it be James Dean... I mean, we're talking about Buddy Holly, a man who, with your group, you were on top of the heap for eighteen months before the tragedy. It wasn't like forever."

Allison: "Seemed like about three weeks. It just zipped by."

Robinson: "Amazing, because very much like James Dean in the movies, he only made three movies, and you people had maybe six or seven hits, and then the tragedy."

Allison: "Yeah, and it's amazing to me the records that are out now that maybe shouldn't even be out. Like the demos we were cutting, and those records are out. Those ones I was talking about in Wichita Falls. Those have all been released now, and I guess they should be, because people want to hear Buddy Holly."

Robinson: "But it's history..."

Allison: "I really wish we'd had more time to do some more, you know. So much happened in the eighteen months, like Buddy and I both got married, which never helps a group. Didn't even help the Beatles. We got married, and boy that changed everything a lot, and Buddy's wife was from New York. He moved to New York, and I guess he moved up there about at the end of '58. We stayed in Texas. I mean, we weren't fighting, I don't know if we wanted to go up there or not, and Norman Petty was telling us, 'You guys better go to New York, or you don't have me to manage the group.' We were kids, and we handled everything just like kids. If we had to do it again, then it'd be a lot different."

Robinson: "Buddy was, apparently, from the people that I know in the business, very demanding in the studio, and he could be nasty and stubborn at times over what he believed was right."

Allison: "He was pretty well that way about everything. He certainly knew what he wanted, and he wasn't wishy-washy about anything."

Robinson: "We know in the business, though, that's how you have to be as a performer to get creative."

Allison: "That's right. You can't put everybody's ideas in on everything if you know what you want. He'd stick with what he wanted, and he wasn't good at compromising. It's hard for me to compare him as far as working in the studio because we were friends, and we hung out after school. We would say, 'How can we make it? How can we not just play here in town?' He was concerned about a three-piece group and it's really easy with a three-piece group, you all get in one car, and you get one room with a rollaway. Holly and I played quite a few dance jobs around Lubbock, just the two of us. He was more of a friend; it wasn't like working for him but working with him, and we'd sit out and say, 'How can we get on the road? How can we be popular?' We thought when we cut that first record on Decca that having a record out made you a star and all of a sudden they'd be calling for gigs. We found out that wasn't the deal! You got to have somebody playing it and buying it as well."

Norman along with his wife Vi recalled stories of how particular Buddy was in the studio, as he would go through microphone after microphone with settings being changed on each one until he found the exact microphone that gave him the exact sound he was looking for. Many stated how laser focused Buddy was, and he knew what he wanted. Although he may have been difficult to work with, he produced hit record after hit record. Rolling Stone Magazine ranked Buddy Holly #13 in the list of the 100 Greatest Artists. He was married to Maria Elena Santiago, who was pregnant at the time of his death. She then miscarried due to psychological trauma.

The following 1957 interview with Holly took place backstage at the Georgia Auditorium for the biggest record star show with Robinson.

Robinson: "The Show of Stars for 1957 featured the changing appearance of rock and roll. The lineup for this event included Buddy Holly and the Crickets, Frankie Lymon and the Teenagers, Frankie Avalon, George Hamilton IV, Buddy Knox and Jimmy Bowen and the Rhythm Orchids, Don and Phil Everly, Paul Anka and Eddie Cochran. Anyone even remotely interested in rock and roll today, we can appreciate the significance of the show, even by today's standards. It was big, the lineup was not only impressive in its day—it was historic! I was most anxious to meet Buddy Holly. The Show of Stars was held on October 23rd, 1957. Buddy Holly and the Crickets had their first hit right up the charts to number three in August of 1957, the song was "That'll Be the Day." In those early days of rock and roll, the disc jockeys such as myself who loved the music would listen to every single new release, and I mean both sides. I liked "That'll Be the Day" and had played it for months before it ever made a mark on the national charts. In those days, Cashbox Magazine had a page filled with Top 10 records from various DJs in North America, and I was one of the few Canadians on that page. I listed "That'll Be the Day" on my Top 10 Hit List for six weeks running. Holly told me that it was my listing of the song that brought it to the attention of other radio stations in North America.

Holly: "Hello, Red, how are you?"

Robinson: "I missed that phone call we had from Toronto at that time."

Holly: "Yeah, we couldn't get together on that."

Robinson: "I'd just like to tell you right now that's your song "Peggy Sue" that you do on a solo there on Coral Records. Is it Coral in the state too?"

Holly: "Yes, it is."

Robinson: "Yeah, it's doing real well, it's number seven song here, and that's lucky number seven, as we say."

Holly: "That's fine."

Robinson: "How long have you had The Crickets together, Buddy?"

Holly: "Since January."

Robinson: "When did you decide to form a group? Was it at that time?"

Holly: "Well, the drummer and I have been playing together for about four years, and we got the other two boys and asked them if they'd like to join us and form a group."

Robinson: "You write your own material, is that right?"

Holly: "Yes, that's right."

Robinson: "Who helped you with "That'll Be the Day"?"

Holly: "Jerry Allison, the drummer."

Robinson: "Where are you all from? Where's your home?"

Holly: "Lubbock, Texas."

Robinson: "Would you like to go back there?"

Holly: "Sure would!" (laughs)

Robinson: "What's the weather like this time of year down there?"

Holly: "Oh, it's not quite this cool. It's not, and it's a little bit drier."

Robinson: "Right now, I'm going to put you on the spot, as I asked you before and I didn't have a microphone with me, what do you think about rock and roll music? Do you think it's on the wane, or what?"

Holly: "I think it's going out quite a bit in the states."

Robinson: "How far down south?"

Holly: "DEEP!" (laughs)

Robinson: "How long do you think it will last, another six months, seven months…?"

Holly: "Oh, possibly, yeah, I think so."

Robinson: "After Christmas, things may change a bit, though."

Holly: "They might pick back up, but I rather doubt it."

Robinson: "Well, we would like to congratulate you here in a special way because the west coast here is sort of responsible for "That'll Be the Day" to get it started out here."

Holly: "Yeah, that's what I heard!"

Robinson: "We're all real happy about it here. Phil Rose of Coral Records in Apex and Brunswick and Eastern Canada was trying to get through to us with you on the phone back there, how was your engagement?"

Holly: 'It was real fine. They received us real well there."

Robinson said from the moment Buddy Holly and he met, there was a bond between them. He was a country boy with much enthusiasm and was happy to have a hit and was intent on adding to that success. When he asked Buddy what song he had coming out next, Holly answered, they had recently finished the track, "Oh Boy," which would go on to a be a Top 10 hit on the Billboard in late 1957.

Robinson: "How do you think it compares with the others?"

Holly: "I like "Oh Boy" better than "That'll Be the Day.""

Robinson: "Really, you think it's better."

Holly: "Of course, I'm no judge."

Robinson: "It's always the listeners that decide the fate of a record. We'd like to congratulate you, and I think you got a good future in the business. One other question, Buddy. If trends changed, would you hop on the trend and go into the other or would you just give up?"

Holly: "I'd hop on the trend, because I'd prefer singing a little bit something a little more quieter anyway."

Robinson: "What do you like down in Texas where you come from? How far is that from a place like Dallas or Crystal City? I mean, Texas is big, man!"

Holly: "Our hometown Lubbock is two hundred and eighty miles straight west of Dallas."

Robinson: "It's been real wonderful talking to you backstage here, Buddy, and I guess your act goes on pretty soon."

Holly: "Yes, it does."

Robinson: "How many numbers?"

Holly: "We do three. We'll do "Ready Teddy," our new song "Oh Boy," and "That'll Be the Day.""

Red Robinson referred to Buddy Holly as a diamond in the rough. In a photo Red had taken with him, Robinson stated, "You can see that his teeth were in poor shape and the glasses he wore were really not as stylish as they might be. It didn't matter to the audience that night, the music of The Crickets filled the hall, and Buddy Holly was recognized by the crowd as something original." The Crickets opened with Sonny Curtis as the lead vocalist for Waylon Jennings concerts for many years.

It was Holly's different sound that grabbed your attention. At times, he would toss in a couple grunts from the man who inspired him, Elvis Presley. Buddy embraced this sound.

Red Robinson was on the air at KGW in Portland, Oregon when the news came across the wire regarding the plane crash. Robinson, like so many others, was hit hard by the news, as he felt somewhat responsible for launching Holly due to his part in playing his first record.

At the age of sixteen, Buddy wrote an essay that included this sentence: "I have thought of making a career out of western music if I am good enough, but I will just have to wait and see how that turns out." To use a song title of his; Buddy, I would say it has been, "Well…Alright."

His body was found near the wreckage. He was wearing a yellow leather-like jacket. According to the autopsy report, his personal effects included $193 in cash, two cufflinks, silver half-inch balls having a jeweled band, and the top portion of a ballpoint pen.

He was laid to rest on Saturday February 7th, which over a thousand people attended. Maria Elena did not attend the funeral and has said on the record that she blames herself for not going.

Buddy Holly is buried in Lubbock Cemetery in Texas. Visiting the grave site is as easy as one could imagine. You simply make the first right upon entering Lubbock Cemetery, and you will see a wood sign with an arrow that states, "Buddy Holly Grave Site" with an arrow to walk across the driveway, where you will find his final resting place. You will notice his name is spelled correctly on the grave but not on the sign.

At the top of the headstone is a set of musical notes that immediately got my attention, as they seemed intentionally put on there and not to be just random notes. After asking around for someone to read them for me, I was informed that the first is a "B Flat" chord, which, I was told, is challenging to play, especially for beginners, and is referred to as the "Happy Chord." His first single, "That'll Be the Day" is in "A" riff, which these very well could be the chords, as he sang the song in four main chords, and "B Flat" is one of them.

Instructional videos do shortcuts so it sounds the same as the song, but many people cannot play it like Buddy did. His father Larry, who passed in 1985 and his mother Ella, who passed in 1990, are buried to his right.

On Holly's 75th birthday, he received a Hollywood star on the walk of fame, which is located outside of Capitol Records.

Trademark Glasses
Buddy Holly Center

Buddy was recognizable for his horn-rimmed spectacles that became his image. At age fourteen, he was told he needed glasses after a school eye test. He suffered from severe nearsightedness, with vision of 20/800 in both eyes. He was originally against wearing glasses and started with a subtle brow line pair. Through peer encouragement, he learned to embrace them, as his friends told him to make a statement about them if he was going to wear them.

His optometrist Dr. Jesse Armistead spotted his signature frames on vacation in Mexico City, made by Faiosa. When they were unable to get Faiosa frames, he would use replacements for Sidewinder or Freeway frames that were similar, made by Shuron. After moving to New York, Buddy bought a pair of Faiosa from Courmettes and Gaul in Manhattan, which were the pair he was wearing on February 3rd.

Buddy's signature glasses were not listed among his personal effects. They were considered lost until the spring after, when the snow melted. They were found, along with a couple of watches, one belonging to the Big Bopper, by a farmer. The other belonged to Holly and was a white gold Omega watch with over forty diamonds that was valued at $5,000 in 1959, which in 2024 would be around $54,000. He handed them over immediately to the Cerro Gordo County Sheriff's Office, where they sat filed away in a manila envelope for twenty-one years! On the outside of the envelope was written 'Charles Hardin Holley, received April 7th, 1959.' The envelope was taken to the county courthouse and got filed away in a filing cabinet. Twenty-one years later, Sheriff Jerry Allen opened the envelope on February 29th, 1980, in the courthouse basement when he was going through old cabinets. The glasses were returned to Maria Elena Holly. She sold them in 1998 for $80,000. Today, they are on display at the Buddy Holly Center in Lubbock, Texas.

The glasses were new to fashion and gave Holly his self-expression. The 1981 MCA album of his Love Songs had nothing on the cover except a pair of black, hornrimmed glasses.

Wearing glasses opened the door for other musicians to create their own style, such as John Lennon and Roy Orbison. Elton John wanted to be like Holly and wore all kinds of unique frames on stage over his many years of performing, and even Elvis Costello wore these glasses as part of his look, and dressing like him throughout his career.

Actor Jeff Goldblum and even Kate Winslet have donned a pair of Buddy frames in recent years. There are several stories of musicians going out shopping for a pair of hornrimmed glasses like those Buddy was wearing. Where others were told not to wear their glasses on stage, they did anyway because Buddy was wearing them.

Today, these frames have become a vivid part of rock and roll history. A few miles north of Taos, NM, artist Steve Teeters constructed a giant metal set that is six feet long that peer out onto New Mexico route 150. Teeters made two pairs; one was black and one rusty for the Buddy Holly Center. The center picked the black pair that are five feet high and thirteen feet wide. This style has since become known as the Buddy Holly Glasses, and you can get frames just like Buddy today.

Some are known by single names like Elvis, Madonna, or Elton, but Buddy is known simply by those black, horn-rimed frames.

The Buddy Holly Center is a historical site that combines art and music. They have collected, preserved, and promoted artifacts of artists and musicians from West Texas, along with the legacy of Buddy Holly. You will find Buddy's glasses that he was wearing that tragic evening on display, guitar picks, and even a pair of his tennis shoes that look like an early pair of Converse. Holly's guitar was being prepared for the center and was partially dismantled for cleaning and polishing, when two guitar picks were discovered under the pickguard, which had slipped underneath and had been there almost a half century!

The center features a West Texas Walk of Fame, which is focused on a Buddy Holly statue that stands eight and a half feet tall and was created Grant Speed. This can be found inside The Buddy and Marie Elena Holly Plaza just west on the corner of Crickets Avenue and 19th St. The Buddy Holly Statue was dedicated on September 5th, 1980 as part of the Walk of Fame that saw its first inductee on the same day in Waylon Jennings. It is loaded with high profile artists who have been inducted, and their plaques are displayed. These include the likes of Buddy Knox, Tanya Tucker, The Crickets, Roy Orbison, "Snuff" Garrett, Bob Montgomery, and Sonny West. Upon walking through the fence to the walk of fame, you will find to your left the "McCartney Oak," due to his historic concert in Lubbock on October 2nd, 2014, and his admiration of Holly.

Tours are available of the Jerry Allison's house, where he lived as a teenager and where he wrote the hit "That'll Be the

Day" in the master bedroom, although this was the country and western version of the song, and Peggy Sue was written in Jerry's bedroom. Please visit:
\https://ci.lubbock.tx.us/departments/buddy-holly-center

Richard Valenzuela
AKA Ritchie Valens (17)

A Mexican Indian American, born on May 13th, 1941. His parents were Joseph Valenzuela and Concepcion (Connie) Reyes.

His father, Steve, was a tree surgeon, trained horses, and was very fond of Ritchie's musical talents. He passed away at age fifty-eight after suffering from a combination of diabetes, alcoholism, and years of traumatic injuries from his career.

His parents divorced in 1944.

The family lived on Filmore St in Pacoima, CA in a tiny home. Ritchie lived in several places and at times could say he was a nomad. After his parents split, he went to live with his father, where he and his brother Bob made a bedroom in a concrete cellar and even stayed with his aunts and uncles in different towns, but most of the time he stayed with his Aunt Ernestine and Uncle Lelo Reyes.

Ritchie had an admiration for The Singing Cowboys of Saturday matinee movies. His father encouraged him to play guitar and trumpet, and he taught himself the drums. Once he learned how to play the guitar, he took it everywhere he went.

A close friend of Valens was Gail Smith, who was also the head of the Ritchie Valens Fan Club. She first saw him when she was around twelve years old when she lived next to a field, and every day after school Ritchie would walk alone across the field, playing his guitar and singing. She stated, "He was different and bold." She was not sure if she ever told him this, as the first time she ever met him was August 8th at a roller rink. Smith told me he was an unforgettable person.

One thing she did point out was at school when he was singing, everyone wasn't running around him as depicted in the movie. She never saw a crowd around him, maybe three or four of his friends were all.

The fan club was started after his death when she started working for Del-Fi records at age thirteen doing record promotion. Bob Keane came up with the idea, and it was active for about four to five years, but Smith still to this day gets contacted about the club.

His guitar was bought at a pawn shop and was bronze. He had a wood shop class in high school, and the color of the day was green. He took the guitar and sanded and sprayed it, which has become the signature color of the Valens Collection. The Grammy Museum in Los Angeles, CA houses the guitar.

On January 31st, 1957, at fifteen years old, he attended Pacoima Junior High and was at the funeral of his grandfather, when the Pacoima mid-air collision occurred that day. A Douglas DC 7B, a four-engine commercial airline, collided with US Air Force Northrop F89 Scorpion jet Interceptor as they were undergoing test flights in a cloudless sky. The DC7B wreckage scattered onto the schoolyard while students were at recess, killing several students, including one of Ritchie's close friends, and injuring over seventy others, with twenty-three being hospitalized. A six-year-old boy was struck by debris while playing in front of his house and was injured, as was a man who suffered from minor injuries who was at a church that was hit by a piece of debris. Due to this, Ritchie would have recurring nightmares of dying in a plane crash, which led to his fear of flying.

Smith recalls this mid-air collision, as it happened right outside the window she was sitting by. She vividly recalls hearing the explosion in the air, debris began to fall, then hot gasoline. She saw the motor falling into the playground on fire and thought they were being bombed. Everyone was scared and got under their desks. The one Gail got under was open on the other side, so she watched out the window.

"We all thought we were going to die." She didn't fly until 1986, stating, "I knew I'd die if I did." She hasn't gotten over this, as the students suffered terribly, and Valens' plane crash happened just months later.

Valens was discovered by Gilbert Rocha, who had his own band in 1957 called "The Silhouettes." Rocha explains that his band had five guys at that time. He was looking for a couple more and was told by his drummer that there was a kid at the school who could play the guitar really well. A couple days later, there was a knock at his door, and this baby-faced kid was standing there with a guitar and a little amp. Rocha thought to himself, Oh boy, this is going to be good. He invited Valens in, and when he started playing, he knocked him off his feet he was so damn good!

Doug Macchia was an aspiring music promoter (a printer by day), and Bob Keane was a client who needed business cards for his new company, Del-Fi Records, told by Corey Long in his book Come on, Baby, Just Rock, Rock, Rock. One day, he told Keane about Valens. Keane first heard Ritchie on May 10th, 1958 at Rennie's Theater in San Fernando. Ritchie had won the talent competition for the third straight week. Keane stated, "I want that singer to come to the studio, we really like him." Valens went to the studio and signed on May 28th, 1958. He began recording immediately.

Bob Keane

Bob Keane, who was Valens' producer and manager, was born Robert Kuhn but changed his name to Keane and at times used Keene in 1970. He became the manager of Pinoy star, Josephine Roberto, who was known as Banig.

As a youngster, he played the clarinet and had an outlook to front a big band like his idol Benny Goodman. At age sixteen in 1938, this became a reality, with his very first show ever at Glendale Junior High School (CA). Due to a canceled show, he was approached by someone at radio station KFWB out of Los Angeles to broadcast his concert. The day after, an agent from MCA who listened to his show wanted to sign him. They billed Keane as "The World's Youngest Bandleader."

After enlisting in the US Air Force and then retiring due to a lung infection, he became the conductor on the Hank McCune radio show.

He met John Simas in 1955, who urged him to start his own record label, which became Keen Records. He went on to sign Sam Cooke to a three-year deal, which saw "You Send Me" reach number one in November of 1957. Bob only had a verbal agreement with Simas and received a letter asking him to invest $5,000 in the company to remain a partner. This he simply did not have and realized he had been fooled into finding a hit record so he could be pushed out of the company.

Keane's wife then urged him to start a new label and find someone else who had been tricked by Simas to put up the money. Del-Fi was created in 1957 from the Greek God of Music, Delphi. His first release was "Caravan" by Henri Rose. The Warner Brothers offered Bob $8,000 for Rose's contract, which he accepted and immediately bought out his partner.

Del-Fi later released the popular song, "Hippy Hippy Shake" by Chan Romero. In 1964, under a subsidiary label created just for The Bobby Fuller Four called Mustang Records, he released the big hit "I Fought the Law" in 1966.

Del-Fi closed in 1967, and Keane went into selling burglar alarm systems to celebrities and oversaw the music careers of his two sons. 1994 saw two Del-Fi records by The Lively Ones and The Centurians, used in the movie Pulp Fiction, which resurfaced Del-Fi. They released CDs of their original material and even signed a few artists. The Del-Fi catalog was sold in 2003 to Warner Brothers Music Group.

Keane died on November 28th, 2009 from kidney failure due to non-Hodgkins Lymphoma. He was eighty-seven.

Keane was played by actor Joe Pantoliano in the movie La Bamba which is now being looked into for a possible remake by Sony Pictures.

When Valens auditioned for Keane, he played an instrumental song which he was asked to make up lyrics for. The result was "Come on Let's Go," an instant hit across the Los Angeles area in the summer of 1958. The title came from his mother, as this was her saying to him all the time and was inspiration for the song.

It was the first recording session at Gold Star Recording Studio in Hollywood, CA, which was a demo studio where you could rent studio time for $15/hour. In 1958, an addition was built, with a larger studio and an echo chamber, which they became known for. Hit records such as "I Got You Babe" by Sonny and Cher, and "You've Lost That Loving Feeling" by The Righteous Brothers were recorded in the studio.

Keane suggested he shorten his name to Valens in order to avoid any prejudice from the name of Valenzuela, and in August, the song was released nationally and sold a halfmillion copies. Ritchie appeared in the movie Go Johnny Go!, Dick Clark's American Bandstand on December 27th, and joined the Winter Dance Party Tour with singles "Donna" and "La Bamba," which were moving up the Top 10 on the record charts.

According to Smith, Valens told her he was most excited to meet The Big Bopper on the tour and did his impression of Hellooo, Baaby! Ritchie was the most popular artist on tour at the time.

In the fall of '58, Ritchie dropped out of school due to the demands of his career, as his popularity skyrocketed overnight. An interesting fact about Valens is that his entire career from the time he was discovered till his death was only eight months long!

Valens didn't write lyrics down on paper and would memorize a couple lines and lyrics. He didn't sing anything the same way twice. The kids called him, "Little Richard of San Fernando." He wrote twenty-two of the thirty-three songs he recorded, which was unheard of at the time, especially for someone that young. He is considered the first Latino to successfully cross over into mainstream rock with three hits in a row: "Come On Let's Go," "Donna," and "La Bamba." "La Bamba" was recorded in Spanish and became a hit internationally!

According to Rocha, Ritchie had a personality where you loved him the minute you met him. He constantly had a big smile on his face, loved to laugh, was smart, and had a loud voice.

His hit songs "La Bamba" and "Donna" were released on the same record, with "Donna" as the A side and "La Bamba," like "Chantilly Lace," was originally the B side on that record.

Donna Ludwig was his high school sweetheart from 1957 until his death. Ludwig states, "I met Ritchie when I was fifteen at a car club party and started dating him." The first time she heard the song was on the telephone as Ritchie sang it to her. Valens told her that he wrote a song for her and didn't tell her he was going to record it. About a couple of months later, Ludwig was driving down the street with all her friends, and the song came on the radio. She admitted that it was a strange feeling. She didn't see him for the rest of the summer until they went back to school, and they once again started seeing one another. Like Rocha, Ludwig shared that everybody liked Ritchie. When I asked Smith about how he handled his popularity, she answered that he wasn't impressed with himself and was cool about it. That he was gracious, grateful, and quiet but was funny and a peacemaker. She told a story about two car clubs getting ready to fight one another and Ritchie stopping it from happening. She told me, "To this day, I have not met anyone who was as kind and gentle as Ritchie."

He performed a school assembly that was held at Pacoima Jr. High School in the auditorium on December 10th, 1958, which was filled with students and held at that time around 725-740 people. Due to a fire around 2008, it has been redone and today only seats 714. The reason for this assembly came from Gail's journalism class, in which they were looking for ideas on how to boost yearbook sales. She suggested that she contact her friends to have the concert, and everyone who bought a yearbook gained free entry into the show.

There is a vinyl record "Ritchie Valens in concert at Pacoima Jr. High" on Del-Fi. The actual show lasted about ninety minutes, with an additional act performing. All the screaming heard on the record was added by Keane for effect, as Smith states the students just clapped after each song. I feel he was Richard Valenzuela off stage, with an alter ego of Ritchie Valens on stage. Valens didn't stay long afterward, as Keane was there with him and took him away, aka "Valens has left the building."

The record includes Smith having a conversation with Valens and the tracks "Come On, Let's Go," "Donna," an Eddie Cochran song, "Summertime Blues," an instrumental called. "From Beyond," and of course "La Bamba." The second side of the record is fascinating, with Bob Keane narrating about five different tracks that Ritchie had recorded at his home. Many had no names, were not finished, and never released. These songs had potential to all be hits, and with Valens, they probably would have been. Just hearing them really hits home regarding how much America lost with these icons and legends.

Valens gave inspiration from his songs "Donna" and "La Bamba" for the groups Los Lobos, The Rascals, R.E.M., and artists like Freddy Fender, Trini Lopez, and even Bob Dylan. "La Bamba" was the model for The Isley Brothers' 1961 hit "Twist and Shout."

Speaking with Connie Valens, who is from California though Iowa is now her home, as Shoeless Joe asked Ray Kinsella in Field of Dreams, I asked, "Is this heaven?"

Connie said, "It is." She explained that she just didn't ever feel like California was the right place for her, but Iowa had wrapped its arms around her.

The younger sister of nine years to Ritchie, Connie was eight years old at the time of the crash. I found her to be a beautiful, grounded person who said when she hears the name Ritchie, she immediately thinks, That's my brother. "He was a father figure who cared for and took care of us. He was driven at just seventeen years old and had no background in music."

Ritchie was Carlos Santana's idol, and he would come across the border if Valens was playing in a border town to see him play.

The youngest brother to Ritchie, Mario, was just eighteen months old when the crash occurred and is now a blues harmonica rocker. Connie urged him to play some of Ritchie's songs, and he told her that he didn't want to play "La Bamba." Connie told him, "You don't have to play "La Bamba," how about "That's My Little Suzie" or "Ohh, My Head!" When people think of Ritchie Valens, just as Mario did, they typically go to the song "La Bamba," when there is a bigger volume to his catalog of music. The track, "Boogie with Stu" by Led Zepplin was inspired from Valens' hit, "Ooh, My Head." Take a listen and you can hear how similar they are. Zepplin recorded the track in 1971 at Headley Garage. They failed to credit Valens or Keane and instead they attributed Mrs. Valens. A lawsuit was filed by The Ritchie Valens Estate in which half of the settlement that was done out of court went to Concha although she was not part of the lawsuit.

A few months passed, and Mario was playing at the Santa Cruz Fairgrounds and played his older brother's "That's My Little Suzie" to the delight of sisters Irma and Connie, who were jumping up and down, crying, clapping, and laughing, as this was the beginning of him playing Ritchie's music.

Connie reported to Brooke Wohlrabe of The Sentinel, the 1987 movie, La Bamba brought the Valenzuela family closer, as they had not been able to share each other's pain in 1959, as the family had never discussed Ritchie or the accident after it happened.

Connie stated, "They did a really good job" with the movie portraying Ritchie. La Bamba is the highest grossing Latino film, grossing over $100 million and was selected in 2017 for preservation in the National Film Registry by the Library of Congress.

George Thorogood, a musician himself from Wilmington, Delaware, who is known for his high-energy sound that hit the 1980s rock radio, told me his very first awareness of Ritchie Valens was in 1983-84 in Santa Cruz, CA. He had heard his music before and knew the tune, "Come On, Let's Go," but when the plane crashed, he was quite young and learned about him much later. He met many members of the Valenzuela family. Concha, Bob, and the entire family was backstage at a Los Lobos concert, as they were just starting out. He stated, "They are all nice people."

They talked to him about a movie script they were trying to push and asked Thorogood if he could help get it in motion.

He was flattered that they even asked him and thought, Why me? He explained, "I'm no Warren Beatty, George Lucas, or Steven Spielberg and know nothing about the movie industry." He understood the angle, though, as anyone connected to some aspect of show business may know people, and he agreed to do anything he could to help, as at that time George was reading scripts himself.

After the movie La Bamba was released, which he feels is a classic, he and Lou Diamond Phillips became, as he stated, "chummy" for a few years. Phillips gifted Thorogood the jacket he wore on stage in the movie, although he didn't keep it very long and went back to Lou and told him that the movie was one of his biggest achievements and one of his children should have the jacket. He gave it back, as Thorogood would have just put it in his closet. As George tells it, Phillips admitted he picked up a few tricks along the way from a slide guitarist from Delaware on how to play a rock star.

When Connie was in her thirties, her mother suggested listening to one of his albums. After the record began playing and hearing his voice, she started to cry and told her mother that she was sorry but just couldn't listen to it. Connie admitted to holding onto hope that he may still be alive and even went as far as thinking somebody from Iowa found Ritchie and he didn't remember who he was. "That's what I told myself," she stated.

Ritchie loved his family. His mother got him to play at the local American Legion, which would be too late for Connie and Irma to attend and they figured they would have to stay home, but their mother wanted them to be there. When the show was over, they had fallen asleep just off the stage area and recall the feeling of Ritchie picking them up and kissing them on their heads to take them home. The American Legion show was made possible by his mother Concepcion "Concha" Reyes, who used the rent money to get the hall. There is a letter that was written by Concha dated February 3rd, 1959, which has been verified as being real from Connie. There is no way to know if this letter was mailed or not. As Connie told me, "I can't honestly explain this. It's possible she wrote this before she found out. Mama liked to write or send cards to stay in touch with her friends and Ritchie's fans, as we did not have a phone."

The eerie writing from Concha states, "Ritchie won't be home for a long while, so I hope I'll have to go and see him, because after two weeks, I start missing him a lot." The letter is signed, The best of luck, Mrs. Connie Valens.

In a 2009 interview on Project Coda, twenty-five years after La Bamba Bob Morales, the older brother to Ritchie said, "I seen my mom age fifteen years in two days." His biggest regret was he never told Ritchie that he loved him.

His body was found ten to twenty feet from the wreckage, wearing a black wool coat by Harris and Frank, a black wool cloth suit by Sobel's and a white shirt. On his right forearm was a tattoo with the initials R.V.

According to the autopsy report, his personal effects included -a silver crucifix and a religious medal, a brown leather pocket case with black lacing and stamped design, numerous receipts, several photos, $22.15 in cash and a check from the Hollywood office for $50 that was noted: 'advance as per contract', and a silver bracelet chain with the word "Donna" attached.

Valens received his first two checks, according to Rocha; one was for $2100 and the other for $1500. He cashed the $2100 check and gave it to his mother so she could put a down payment on a house in 1958 at 13428 Remington Street in Pacoima, California. The family owned the home for thirty years but only lived in it for seven, as it was just too hard. From a recent visit, the home has seen better days, but you can feel the history, standing in front of a white picket fence that was added after Valens lived there.

On January 19th, 1959, he threw a party for all his friends at his mother's new house as a going away party. Smith attended and explained that people were in the garage and it wasn't a loud gathering but rather laid back, but people were dancing, as her mother and Connie were best friends. She recalls the song "16 Candles" playing, and Valens showed up around halfway through the party.

The night before he left, Gail went to church with her mother, along with Ritchie and Concha. At mass, they were in the church pew, on their knees, and she states, "Leaning shoulders on each other," which she can still feel. "It was an amazing experience."

After mass, they both sat in the backseat, and she asked Ritchie, "How can you go?"

He replied, "They make me fly everywhere." Smith then told him that she heard it was snowing back there, and she was worried about a plane. Valens said," Don't worry about me. If we crash, I will land on my guitar in the snow and use it as a sled!"

He left the next day for Chicago, and on January 21st, he joined the Winter Dance Party in Milwaukee, WI.

There was no visitation for Ritchie, but the Friday before the funeral, they all prayed the rosary at home. His services were held on Saturday, February 7th. He was carried to the cemetery in a copper-colored hearse and is buried at San Fernando Mission Cemetery in Mission Hills, California. Visiting the grave, it is something to stand there and look down at the headstone, buried next to his mother. You get a sense that you are standing by greatness that was taken too soon.

Valens was the first rock star to come from the west coast. The Ritchie Valens Memorial Highway is a stretch on the I-5 Freeway between state Routes 170 and 118 freeways. The home, junior high school, and grave site are all within about ten minutes of one another and should be visited.

Ritchie has a star on the Hollywood Walk of Fame that was unveiled on May 11th, 1990, which was only two days before his 49th birthday. The family had to raise the money for the star at 6733 Hollywood Boulevard. La Bamba stars Lou Diamond Phillips and Esai Morales were in attendance.

Valens was inducted into the Rock and Roll Hall of Fame in 2001 and has his own postage stamp. The Ritchie Valens name is trademarked by the family. He may be gone, but he is not forgotten in the Pacoima, CA area, as there are murals to honor his legacy, such as the side of the Pacoima Middle School, painted by artist Manuel Velasquez, the intersection of Van Nuys and Amboy Avenue by Hector Ponce, and Levi Ponce painted a mural at the intersection of Van Nuys and Telfair Avenue along with one at Pacoima Junior High School.

When Ritchie bought the home for his mother, they were at the pinnacle of his life without realizing it. He has been bringing people together for decades and made a big impact in such a short time.

Smith said, "Can't ever forgot him, ever!" She believes he has made the greatest impact on her life and is still with her in everything she does. Ritchie changed her life, as he influenced her deeply. The assembly changed her. She was a skinny, buck-toothed, shy, naïve, little girl that he accepted for who she was. He cared for her, spent time with her, and even went out of his way for Gail. He gave her courage and told jokes when she was terrified, as her voice was shaking at the start of the concert, not having done anything like it before.

As she puts it, "I wouldn't have experienced life if it wasn't for Ritchie."

He was achieving his dreams of ending poverty for his family. He purchased a house, had a beautiful girl, success, and a future. A seventeen-year-old boy who some may say came from the wrong side of the tracks said, "Come On, Let's Go! We Belong Together."

Pilot Roger Arthur Peterson
(21)
& Pilot Training

A forgotten name in this tragic event. Roger Peterson was born in Alta, Iowa on May 24th, 1937. He was the first of four children to Arthur Erland Peterson, a farmer, and Pearl I. Kraemer Peterson. He grew up in a converted one-room schoolhouse on the family farm. He attended Fairview Consolidated School and graduated in 1954. His graduation class was just seven students, in which only two were girls. He played on the only two sports teams that were offered by the school—baseball and basketball—and was the class vice president his senior year.

Peterson worked as a construction worker and drove a truck after high school before joining the National Guard.

His father owned a small airplane and he had been flying since he was around nine or ten years old. He was issued a commercial pilot's certificate with an airplane single engine land rating, which means it only lands on land and has a single engine. At the time of his death, he had an application in at Northwest Airlines.

Barb Dwyer said, "He was such a nice, clean looking, nice looking, clean-cut young man."

Jerry backed this up, adding," Good looking, smart kid."

Roger was employed by Dwyer Flying Service for one year as a commercial pilot and flight instructor. Dwyer Flying Service carried the tagline "Your Friendly CESSNA dealer" and opened in 1953 as a charter flying, student instruction, aircraft maintenance, and sales company. Roger had been flying since 1954, had over seven hundred flying hours with approximately fifty-two hours of dual instrument training, and passed his written exam but failed the instrument flight check the previous year. He was not yet qualified to fly in weather that required flying solely by reference to instruments. Roger had around 128 hours on this type of airplane (Bonanza Beechcraft) but zero of his instrument training was for this aircraft. Basically, all his time flying the Bonanza aircraft was for charter flights

In February of 1958, he enrolled in the Graham Flying School in Sioux City for only a couple of months. Lambert Fletcher from Hartley, IA in 1958 gave Peterson his instruction on dual flight instruments. "Mr. Peterson was below average at the end of this time in that he had tendencies up into the 6th hour of developing severe vertigo and allowing the aircraft to go into diving spirals to the right." (Lehmer, 1997) In March of 58, he failed phase III of Instrument Rating Flight Test. According to Melvin Wood of Graham Flying, Roger would become confused and was not able to start a course and had lost control of the plane on two separate occasions when he would be trying to read charts and then descend below the altitude he was supposed to be at. He also said that he was "very susceptible" to being easily distracted and got agitated as well as confused during his flight testing.

His last Civil Aviation Authority (CAA) 2nd class physical was on March 29th, 1958. A hearing deficiency of his right ear was identified, and due to this he was given a flight test. A waiver stating this deficiency was issued on November 29th, 1958.

All his instrument training was taken in several different aircraft, all equipped with the conventional type of artificial horizon and none with the Sperry Attitude Gyro. Roger Peterson was said to not have enough training with flying this model of aircraft to rely solely on instruments. According to many different pilots, ranging from those who fly small planes to those who operate commercial aircraft, flying solely on instruments is something very difficult to master during training, when your body is telling you to go the exact opposite of what the instruments are reading.

According to CAB, Peterson had taken instrument training on airplanes that were equipped with artificial horizon attitude indicators instead of the less common Sperry Attitude Gyro that the Beechcraft was equipped with. The directional gyros. which are directional indicators, were caged. This is so you know which way you are going. Pilot Peterson may have become confused with this plane's gyroscope, which operated in the exact opposite way to the other planes he was comfortable flying, meaning he would have believed he was ascending when in fact he was descending.

He wasn't supposed to fly that night, as there was nothing in the books, but received a call about a charter flight of rock and roll stars. Lehmer reported that Roger's friend and his wife told him not to go on the flight. Roger had called the Air Traffic Service three times in the eight hours prior to take off for the weather forecast for the route after he was assigned to pilot the aircraft. Each time, he was told that the weather had ceilings of 4,200 feet or higher, with visibility of ten miles or more. ATCS did NOT inform Peterson of a "Flash Advisory" of a hundred-mile-wide (160 kilometers) band of snow moving into the area at twenty-five knots (thirteen meters per second). Moderate to heavy icing conditions were present, along with winds of thirty-five to fifty-five miles per hour. When he was taxiing to the runway, he once again radioed for the weather report. The report stated, ceiling three thousand feet, the sky is obscured, visibility six miles, with light snow and winds gusting twenty to thirty-five miles per hour.

What has not been thought about or talked about is Peterson would have had to come back and return home after dropping off the artists. There had to be a discussion about possibly staying in Fargo, North Dakota due to the conditions, but DeAnn Peterson was expecting Roger home by six-thirty the next morning, as they only had one car and she was planning on taking it to work. She ended up getting a ride from a friend. They drove by Dwyer Flying Service, and there was their green Ford Fairlane. She had a premonition it was going to be there and had a feeling that something had happened. By the time Barb Dwyer and her friend Judye McGlothlen arrived at her work, she knew he was gone. They took her to the doctor to get something to calm her down.

Roger was pinned inside the wreckage and had to be extracted.

Peterson's memorial service was held at Redeemer Lutheran Church in Ventura, IA on February 5th, and his funeral was at St. Paul Lutheran on Friday, February 6th in his hometown of Alta, IA. Pilot Peterson is buried at the Buena Vista Memorial Park Cemetery in Storm Lake, Iowa. He was married to his high school sweetheart, DeAnn Lenz on September 14th, 1958 at the same place his funeral was held, and they lived just a few blocks from the Surf Ballroom in the Armsbury Cottage on North Shore Drive. She eventually got married and moved to Minnesota.

Jerry Dwyer stated, "He was one fine young man."

According to the autopsy report, his personal effects included $20 cash and a paycheck from Dwyer Flying Service dated January 21, 1959 for $130.55.

The 1959 Winter Dance Party

Irving Feld from General Artists Corporation (GAC) put the tour together: twenty-one days of one-night shows across the Midwest. The tour manager was Sam Geller from Baltimore, MD.

Larry Lehmer who wrote, The Day The Music Died: The Last Tour of Buddy Holly, the Big Bopper, and Ritchie Valens stated, Holly was paid a weekly salary plus a share of the profits, which meant around $3500 a week for him and his band. Valens was to make around $800 per week. Lehmer continued that there was a European Tour being arranged and Feld, the tour organizer, was to become Buddy's manager, along with Holly making designs for his own recording studio and record pressing plant to be in Lubbock, Texas. On this tour, Holly took to Valens, and there were discussions about Buddy producing a record for Ritchie.

It was nicknamed "The Tour from Hell" by Buddy Holly and his friends. The schedule was brutal, as it zigzagged back and forth across the States. The Winter Dance Party traveled a total of 5,327 total miles on this tour from hell. The distance traveled prior to February 2nd, excluding the canceled Appleton, WI show, would have been 2,182 miles. Keep in mind, these distances were calculated using the modern driving routes, as the Eisenhower Interstate Highway System was still in its infancy in 1959. To put this into perspective, the total mileage of the United States is about 2,800 miles from east to west and 1,650 miles from north to south. This tour, in only three states before Clear Lake, almost traveled the width of the USA! Add on the additional 3,145 miles after the crash over four states, and it would have added up to the equivalent of traveling from one end of the USA and back to the other and could have traveled North and South and back with more to go! Distances from city to city may have changed since 1959 due to new roads etc. and in some cases considerably. (Compliments of Kelly Burgin)

Here is the tour schedule:

Before the crash:

January 23   Milwaukee, WI - Million Dollar Ballroom
January 24   Kenosha, WI - Eagles Ballroom
January 25   Mankato, MN - Kato Ballroom
January 26   Eau Claire, WI - Fournier's Ballroom
January 27   Montevideo, MN - Fiesta Ballroom
January 28   St. Paul, MN - Prom Ballroom
January 29   Davenport, IA - Capitol Theater
January 30   Fort Dodge, IA - Laramar Ballroom
January 31   Duluth, MN - National Guard Armory
February 1 Appleton, WI - Cinderella Ballroom
(canceled)
February 1   Green Bay, WI - Riverside Ballroom
February 2   Clear Lake, IA - Surf Ballroom (this was an add-on show)

*After the Crash:

February 3 Moorehead, MN - Armory
February 4 Sioux City, IA
February 5 Des Moines, IA - Val Air Ballroom
February 6 Cedar Rapids, IA - Danceland Ballroom
February 7 Spring Valley, IL - Les Buz Ballroom
February 8 Chicago, IL - Aragon Ballroom
February 9 Waterloo, IA - Hipprodrome Ballroom
February 10 Dubuque, IA - Melody Hill

February 11 Louisville, KY - Memorial Auditorium
February 12 Canton, OH - Memorial Auditorium
February 13 Youngstown, OH - Stambaugh Auditorium
February 14 Peoria, IL - Armory
February 15 Springfield, IL - Illinois State Armory

*Frankie Avalon, Fabian, and Jimmy Clanton were pulled off other tours to replace Buddy, Ritchie, and the Bopper after the crash. Carl Bunch's bandmate from the group The Poor Boys and Ronnie Smith also joined the tour to help. Bobby Vee performed on February 3rd in Moorehead, MN.

Looking at the tour stops, it gives you an idea of three weeks going all over the Midwest in the worse part of winter. A large portion of the interstates and highways were not even built yet. They were narrow, two-lane, rural highways with snow in places waist deep. They went through five buses, and one even froze up, as they were converted school buses with no heat! They burned newspapers and had to lay on top of each other to stay warm, as temperatures were as low as -30 degrees. The busses had a foul odor due to them not being able to shower or have clean clothes, plus all the garbage that had been built up. Keep in mind, they also had no road crew to help with any setup or tear down and did it all themselves. Carl Bunch, who was the drummer for Buddy Holly, had gotten frostbite and was taken to a hospital and was no longer part of the tour prior to arriving in Clear Lake, which had a population of six thousand at that time and was billed as "Iowa's Fun Capital."

February 2nd was an open date on the schedule. The artists had come from Green Bay, WI, and they were forced to cancel an afternoon show on February 1st in Appleton, WI due to the bus breaking down. JP Richardson, aka Big

Bopper, had a fever and the flu according to Carroll Anderson, who was the manager of the Surf Ballroom. Anderson stated, "They were all tired, freezing, and hungry."

One of the biggest Holly fans in the world is Don Larson, who attended the Winter Dance Party in Eau Claire, WI on January 26th, 1959. He told me that tickets were easy to obtain, and Holly lived up to his high expectations, as he couldn't believe he was coming to his town and was excited to see him. He only went to see Buddy. He went home and before he went to bed he jumped on his mother's typewriter and typed the setlist from the evening. Although they are not in the exact order as he went from his memory, he does recall, "Gotta Travel On" being the first song he sang, which was followed by "Be-Bop-A-Lula" and "Whole Lotta Shakin'" before heading into his signature tracks of "That'll Be the Day" and "Peggy Sue." Don feels he is the only person who wrote down the setlists from the Winter Dance Party Tour. He said he would not be surprised if Holly did the same songs, as Jennings had not played bass guitar before and he would not want him to play songs unfamiliar to him. He does not remember the girls screaming at all.

Larson thought that he would go see him and that the bands would go home afterward, as there was no way of knowing anything about a tour. There wasn't anything about where they were going or where they had been. He told me, "If had known, I would have asked for my parents' permission and would have followed them around." However, he was a seventeen-year-old high school senior and had school the next day.

Don almost met his idol, but the stars did not align. After the show, he and his friend, who was driving, went home. Their normal routine after a football or basketball game or dances was to go to Sammy's Pizza, and the next day on the school bus when his friend was picked up, he sat by him and asked why he didn't go to Sammy's last night.

Larson replied, "Why, what was going on?"

He was told that Buddy Holly, Ritchie Valens, Big Bopper, and Dion and the Belmonts stopped in for pizza.

"Oh My God, Oh My God, Oh My God!" was all he could say.

There was a time when he thought he was the ONLY Buddy Holly fan in the whole world! He explained that he just didn't know anybody.

In 1962, Don started dating a girl who had photos from the Winter Dance Tour. She knew how much of a fan he was of Holly and took them out of her photo album and gave them to him. In 1977, they became world-famous as they were the first ones ever seen on this tragic tour. From these photos, he became friends with Waylon Jennings after having a one-of-a-kind photo blown up to poster size and presenting it to him after one of his shows at the famous Red Rock Amphitheater in Colorado. Larson explained he thought Jennings was going to drop it, as he was visibly shaking looking at it.

John Mueller, leader of the highly acclaimed official tribute show of the Winter Dance Party, tells me, "When we first did the Winter Dance Party, we decided to recreate the order of the 1959 tour. I realized firsthand how exhausting it was, and we were on nice, cushy, fifteen-passenger vans verse the broken-down school buses the rock and rollers were on."

Mueller was physically exhausted and lost his voice by the time they got to the Surf Ballroom. The amount of respect he already had for them grew even higher. In pictures from the 59' tour, they all look happy and were having a great time, but John feels they had to be hurting and understood why Buddy wanted to charter a plane, as he had the same feeling of just wanting to get away from the bus, people, and spend eight hours in a bed. He stated, "It became golden, and I would have done the same thing!" The only route that made sense according to Mueller was the first two days going from Milwaukee, WI to Kenosha, WI, which was only an hour away. The rest were insane, and they stopped after the Surf and later did the rest of the stops, as eleven of them were enough for him.

Surf Ballroom

Clear Lake Iowa is in Cerro Gordo County, with a population of a little over 7,500 according to the most recent census. It's named after a large lake, with several marinas and state parks. It's history dates back, as it was the summer home of the Dakota and Winnebago Native Tribes and features a historic downtown with buildings from the 1890s. Found off the interchange of Interstate 35 and U.S. Highway 18 halfway between the Twin Cities in Minnesota and Des Moines, IA.

Take some time and stop and see this historic site as it was that evening. If you've never been and are in the Clear Lake area, I cannot recommend it enough. The original Surf Ballroom was located across the street from its current location at Witke's Beach, built in 1933 by Carl Fox. It was the old Tom Tom Ballroom and was a wood-framed structure, created to resemble a beach club on the ocean. Just beyond the main entrance, at one time you could find Decker's Hamburger Stand that was connected structurally to the ballroom, although it operated independently. The stand fizzled out by the mid-30s.

The original Surf Ballroom featured an open-air roof garden that was used for outdoor dancing. In this era, ballrooms were the central model for dancing and live music.

Acts such as Count Basie, Glenn Miller, and Tommy Dorsey, among others, were regular performers. Catastrophe struck at two-thirty a.m. on Sunday, April 20th, 1947, when a fire broke out that destroyed the ballroom. Fox and his family were sleeping upstairs in an apartment and were able to escape the blaze. The damage was so bad that any idea of restoring it was quickly erased. Plans for its replacement were quickly underway, and a new Surf Ballroom was rebuilt across the street from the original location. in what was the original venue's parking lot.

The current Surf reopened across the street on July 1st, 1948, with a seating capacity of 2,100 and a 6,300 square-foot dance floor. The ballroom resembles that of an ocean beach club, with murals on the back walls that are hand painted to look like the surf and swaying palm trees. The furnishings inside the Surf Ballroom are bamboo, with the ambiance of a South Sea island. The stage is surrounded by palm trees, and the clouds projected overhead make it seem as if you're dancing outside under the stars! Surf became a "must play" venue in the 50s, with manager Carroll Anderson, who took the helm in 1950, as he attracted the biggest names in music.

The green or dressing room is 14'4"x10' 9", with stage access and a full-length mirror. Whenever an act plays in the Surf Ballroom, it is now tradition for them to sign the wall in the dressing room. There are thousands of names, and just about every available space is filled. Somewhere on the walls are the drawings of Buddy Holly, Ritchie Valens, and The Big Bopper. There are signatures from famous musicians and other notables, including a couple of presidents and a former Secretary of State. Tommy Townsend played the Surf and signed the infamous signature walls of the dressing room toward the top. Don McLean's signature includes, "There are ghosts here."

Artists who have taken that stage, outside of those who perished that night, include the likes of Roy Orbison, Ricky Nelson, Conway Twitty, REO Speedwagon, Alice Cooper, The Doobie Brothers, ZZ Topp, Lynyrd Skynyrd, and countless others, including George Thorogood, who has played the Surf many times before it was renovated, noting the phone that Buddy made his last call on was still in operation at that time.

The stage has three levels. The front of it has a width of thirty-nine feet, mid-stage is thirty-one feet, and the back of stage is twenty feet wide. When the Winter Dance Party came through, the back two tiers where the stage, as the front stage was added years later. Walking from the dressing room up the four steps to stage level one, you can easily imagine what that night would have felt and sounded like, with teenagers crammed up against the small stage.

Today, it features a museum, wall of fame, and a gift shop. The Surfside Lounge, or Cypress Room as it is now called due to the cypress wood on the walls, was not original to the ballroom but came shortly afterward and for a short time was used to serve food. The upcoming Music Enrichment Center will be a descriptive, immersive experience, as it will tell stories of the Winter Dance Party, Surf Ballroom, Carl Fox, and Clear Lake. It is adjacent to the ballroom and slated to open in 2025. Look at these historical dates.

> *January 27th, 2009, The Rock and Roll Hall of Fame Museum located in Cleveland Ohio dedicated the Surf Ballroom as a historic Rock and Roll Landmark.*
> *September 16th, 2011, the Surf Ballroom and Museum is officially listed on the National Register of Historic Places.*
> *January 13th, 2021, The US Department of the Interior designated the Surf Ballroom a natural Historic Landmark, recognizing its enduring role in the history of American Music.*

> *The Surf Ballroom is Iowa's 27th National Historic Landmark.*

The stage in the ballroom is a renowned domain, with all those who have performed on it. A plaque located outside the building contains the line "Surf is the bedrock of where the sound and attitude of rock and roll changed forever."

The Surf contains a set of headphones from the plane that Pilot Peterson was wearing and an authentic Gibson Limited Edition Buddy Holly Model Guitar. The story goes that in the mid-90s, a couple from Mason City placed an old, yellow, plastic bag on Jeff Nicholas's desk, who is the president of the Surf Ballroom and Museum and inside was a headset.

Mel Torkelson's father was a pilot, and they were out at the airport shortly after the crash. Jerry Dwyer said, "Come on, I want to show you something." They walked into a hanger, and the plane was all laid out, reconstructed somewhat, and Jerry picked up the headset and said, "Here, you want this?"

The family had it in their possession ever since.

The North Iowa Cultural Center and Museum was formed for the sole purpose of preserving, maintaining, and managing the Surf Ballroom. The Dean Snyder family of Clear Lake agreed with the North Iowa Cultural Center and Museum Inc. to have the Surf operated as a non-profit organization. The Snyder family bought the ballroom in 1994 with the purpose of preserving it, as it was getting ready to be demolished for a grocery store.

At times, the Surf was an uphill battle to make a profit and has become an important stop for tourists. In the nineties, the Snyder family did research to restore the Surf Ballroom to what it had been during the Winter Dance Party. Back in the

70s, a group of businessmen had bought it, not because they wanted to own a ballroom but didn't want to see it demolished after it had fallen into disrepair. Snyders purchased it from this group.

Jerry Dwyer told Nicholas that this was not Clear Lake's finest hour, and they would have been good with letting it be, but due to the popularity of Buddy Holly, the hit song by Don McLean, the Rolling Stones first cover songs in the United States being Holly's, along with the Beatles naming themselves because of the Crickets, this was just too big of a story to not talk about. Unfortunately, the Surf has been criticized for profiting from a tragedy, when in fact they are not profiting but honoring the music and respecting the individuals. Clear Lake honors these artists with Ritchie Valens Drive, JP Richardson Avenue, and Buddy Holly Place, which is the road to the east side of the Surf. Three Stars Plaza is located a half block from the ballroom, showcasing a piece of art that exhibits a fifteen-foot record player spindle with three 45 records stacked for Holly, Valens, and Richardson. At night, the three records light up in blue neon.

Mayor Crabb stated, "This event in history has made a positive impact on a resort tourist community that features a lake and underwent an extensive twenty-five-million-dollar restoration." He credits radio DJ, "The Mad Hatter" for bringing attention to this town with starting the Winter Dance Party in 1979, which made a difference, as people travel from overseas and worldwide to visit.

Surf Ballroom's Winter Dance party was the idea of Clear Lake's radio DJ Darryl "The Mad Hatter" Hensley from his on-air broadcast in the late 70s on KZEV. It was to be held on February 2nd, 1979, which was the twentieth anniversary of the crash. Wolfman Jack was the emcee and Del Shannon, The Drifters, Jimmy Clanton, The Whitesidewalls, and original Cricket Nikki Sullivan performed. This is now an annual three-day event each year in the first part of February.

February 2nd, 1959 Lineup

The cost for admission to the concert that was set to start at eight p.m. and end at midnight was $1.25 and was said to be for ages twelve to twenty-one. An estimated one thousand teenagers and parents attended the Surf show. The opening act was Frankie Sardo, who had the hit tune "Fake Out," which was listed as "Take Out" on the poster. Bob Hale was the master of ceremonies, as well as for the fiftieth anniversary Winter Dance Party in 2009.

Your mind can try and imagine what the final show may have been like to attend. The number of people who have said to have been there far exceeds the amount of space the ballroom holds. What was the crowd like that night, the vibe? And most importantly, what did the music sound like? After finding a few individuals who have been verified to have been in attendance, they helped paint this picture.

John Wonsmos of Lake Milla, IA, who attended Thornton High School and lived across the street from the schoolhouse, was with a group of friends that had made the decision to go to the movies in Mason City. They arrived early and decided to go cruising around Clear Lake and saw on the marquee at the Surf Ballroom the name Buddy Holly. The majority of the guys were country and western fans, but John and his neighbor asked to be dropped off and the rest would pick them up afterward. Wonsmos expressed that the crowd was enthusiastic, and they had to look up to see the bands on stage.

He raved to his parents how good the show was, and the next day at lunch, he and was told by his mother that the artists had been killed. He felt some sadness, as he saw them on their last performance. He obtained all three of these artists' autographs on a piece of lined notebook paper, which he sold about fifteen years ago to a Boston DJ for $800.00.

The story from Dilla (Niederfrank) Arneson, who is now eighty years old, is hard to forget. She was a fan of the Big Bopper, and a group of girls from nearby Garner, IA would go to the teen dances at the Surf. The parents would take turns taking them and then another would come get them. On this night, it was Dilla's father's turn to pick them up. She described that he was an early to bed, early to rise person and showed up before the show was over because of the snow, causing Dilla and her friends to leave early. She stated, "I was so embarrassed!" They didn't see the end of the concert, as they left probably thirty minutes before it ended. She did recall the weather was bad outside. They sat in the booths at the back of the ballroom.

Like Wonsmos, she also heard about the tragedy at lunch the next day. She worked in the lunchroom distributing the milk, and one of her friends that went with her the night before came through and said, "Did You Hear?" This was the first time she had heard about it.

Mary Charlson, who was fourteen at the time, was a big fan of Dion. She'd heard about the show on the radio, which had been held on a school night, and bought tickets at the door. Mary painted a picture of all the teenagers cramming to get as close to the stage as possible. She recalls everyone singing loud, not screaming. This was the only time she ever saw Dion in person and wished he would come back to the Surf again, though it never happened. She stated that he was as good as she thought he would be.

She heard about the crash the next day on KGLO news and could not believe it, though she had encountered white-out conditions on her way home and had been scared to death.

According to Dion DiMucci, The Big Bopper took the stage after Sardo, followed by Dion and The Belmonts, Ritchie Valens, Buddy Holly, and a finale with them all taking the stage. According to Lehmer, the first set lineup was Frankie Sardo, The Big Bopper, Ritchie Valens, Dion and the Belmonts, and Buddy Holly. After a break, set two had Dion and the Belmonts with Holly playing the drums, who then took the stage and played, "Gotta Travel On," which was followed by "Salty Dog Rag," in which Waylon Jennings joined in on. "Brown Eyed Handsome Man" finished the set as the rest of the band joined in, Bopper the last to come out, carrying his telephone!

Nicholas told me, "During the fifties, many felt that rock and roll was going to ruin their youth, and some believe it did." Crabb vividly remembers Buddy Holly on the television from the Ed Sullivan Show and his mother saying, "Well, Sullivan, this is no place for that."

From Nicholas' understanding, at the Surf on that evening, the dance floor was filled with kids while the parents stood around the edge on the pavilion, up a couple of steps, with their arms crossed, watching to make sure nothing bad was going to happen and the devil didn't show up!

Frank Sardo Aviana And Dion Dimucci

Frankie Sardo

Born September 16th, 1936 in Brooklyn, NY and passed away in 2014 from cancer.

At age of five, he made his first musical debut on stage at the Theatre of Little Italy in the Bronx, NY, where he performed with his parents, who had a comedy act. Sardo acted on stage at Fork Union Military Academy and served in Korea. Upon returning, he and his brother formed a comedy group. His first recording as a singer was for MGM Records in 1958. The follow-up record was "Fake Out," written by his brother Johnny, released by ABC-Paramount, and became a regional hit. He was invited to join the Winter Dance Party of 1959 as the opening act.

From his interview with Blue Days Productions, in which he returned to the Surf Ballroom, he was a self-proclaimed clown and music was fun for him. He stated that everyone had fun on this tour, as they told jokes and sang on the bus. He stated that Ritchie had a terrible cold but was always happy. Sardo said, "Their lives were definitely taken long before their time. That's the tragedy of it." It bothered Sardo that music was fun to him but for those three it was their career, and just like that—they were gone. It is my opinion that this crash finished Frankie Sardo's career, as he carried a level of guilt with him. In his words, "I would rather have the guys back. Take my name out of the database like it never happened."

Sardo shared that he sang, "Classroom" and "Fake Out" that evening and possibly one more tune. He released music until 1962 as a duo with his brother, known as Frankie and Johnny. On September 7th, 1960, he performed his song, "When the Bells Stop Ringing" on American Bandstand.

He was not asked if he wanted to fly and took the bus to Fargo, ND. The crash affected Sardo mentally, as he said he had lost dear friends and upon finding out, he went and sat on the bus in silence.

Frank later became a film actor and producer under the name Frank Avianca. He assisted with the music production for the movie, Hells Angels '69.

Dion DiMucci

Born in the Bronx, NY on July 18th, 1939, Dion started singing at age five. His father introduced him to Paul Whitman, who was a 1920s bandleader and discovered talent. Around the age of twelve, Dion began appearing on radio and television shows with Whitman while also performing with The Fordham Daggers.

He would often sing on street corners. By the age of sixteen, he knew around forty Hank Williams songs.

In 1957, he bought studio time to record four rock and roll songs as a Valentine's Day gift for his mother. The producers of the Teen Club TV Show heard the songs and started promoting them. DiMucci was approached by Irv Spicer of Mohawk Records to record a single. He agreed but insisted on his own backup group, which Spicer agreed to. Dion then formed The Belmonts, which was named after Belmont Avenue where they sang on the corner and consisted of the best singers he knew. In May of 1958, he appeared on Dick Clark's Saturday Night which pushed their careers forward, not to mention the single "I Wonder Why" was the #1 song in the Bronx. According to Dion, he met Buddy in NY at the Alan Freed Show and said Holly took flying lessons at Teterboro Airport in NJ during the fall of 1958.

Their big hit came in 1959, entitled "A Teenager in Love," and they joined the Winter Dance Party.

Dion stated, "The weather was so bad that tree branches were snapping." Valens was freezing, as he had not seen weather like that. He was sick and talked to his mom a lot on the phone. As DiMucci tells the story, on Sunday, February 1st, the bus broke down on Route 51 right outside Ironwood, MI by Pine Lake around four a.m. as a piston rod went through the engine in the middle of nowhere. It was blinding snow, total darkness, and nothing was open. "We started to flag down cars." Carl Bunch had gotten frostbite and was sent out first to a hospital in Ironwood. They had to cancel the show in Appleton and played in Green Bay that night. Buddy played drums for Dion, while Carlo Mastrangelo of The Belmonts played drums for Buddy. According to Dion, Holly loved Mastrangelo and wanted to hire him.

The bus arrived in Clear Lake, IA somewhere between six to seven-thirty p.m. on February 2nd, depending on what source I spoke with or researched. Showtime was set for eight p.m.

They played "All by Myself" as the opener and did other artists' songs such as Jerry Lee Lewis and Fats Domino. Dion explains, "Buddy told me, 'Take care of my guitar, Dion. Take care of my guitar like you do your testicles." Dion passed on the opportunity for a seat on the plane due to the cost and rode the bus to Moorhead, MN, which arrived around ten to ten thirty a.m. on February 3rd. He recalls it being kind of warm and the sun was shining. Locals were watching a black and white television set in the hotel lobby, when it came across that rock and roll stars died in plane crash. He went back to the bus and sat there in a trance. "I was totally, like, in shock. I walked back onto the bus, and I was the only one on the bus. Ritchie's blue outfit was hangin' from the luggage rack, and Buddy's guitar was on the seat, and JP's hat was sitting there. I was alone on the bus. And I was baffled."

Sardo and DiMucci continued till the end of the tour, and he was inducted into the Rock and Roll Hall of Fame in 1989.

The Big Bopper had his biggest hit "Chantilly Lace" and others like "White Lightnin'," "Little Red Riding Hood," and "Purple People Eater Meets the Witch Doctor." Ritchie Valens had a list of great hit records that included "La Bamba," "Come on, Let's Go," "We Belong Together," "Donna," and "Framed." He entertained the crowd before Buddy Holly, as he was the headliner on the tour, and in those days, they only played a handful of songs each night.

Holly left us with a long list of great hit songs, such as "That'll Be the Day," "Everyday," "Peggy Sue," "Rave On," "Ready Teddy," and "Oh Boy!"

The set list is heavily debated, and it is hard to find out exactly what that playlist was that night and in what order the songs were played. Several sites and many individuals have stated that all three headliners; The Big Bopper, Ritchie Valens, and Buddy Holly performed "Brown-Eyed Handsome Man" as the last song of the night. Bob Haley, who was a DJ at KRIB in Mason City, remembered Holly telling the crowd at the

Surf, "Hey, we'd love to do one more, we have a plane to catch. We will be back in the spring for The Spring Dance Party!" (C. Long 2024).

One can only imagine what it may have been like to attend a Winter Dance Party Show in 1959. The stories told, articles written, and interviews given can paint the scene.

After attending John Mueller's Winter Dance Party Tribute Show at The South Point Casino in Las Vegas in October 2024, I had a first-hand look at those who had been teenagers of that era. Watching their faces come alive with wide smiles and eyes full of happiness as the memories of yesteryear raced through their minds. The show, music, and vocals are eerily like the real Buddy, Ritchie, and J.P. Picturing myself at the Surf in '59, I could almost hear these now much older teens cramming the stage to get a glimpse of their rock and roll idols and being filled with excitement as they sang word for word each song, just waiting with eagerness for the next hit to be played. They would have left walking on air, not knowing the next morning they would awake to have that air sucked out of their lungs with the news of the plane crash that killed them all.

Buddy Holly decided to charter a plane. He first tried to arrange a flight from Fort Dodge, IA to Duluth, MN but couldn't make it happen. Bill McCollough, who was twentytwo at the time, was the emcee for the tour stop in Fort Dodge. He had taken flying lessons and after talking with Buddy, who was not happy with being on the bus, off the cuff told Holly to allow him to fly them to the next stop. Holly jumped at this offer, which McCollough quickly backpedaled out of. Holly then asked him to call someone who could fly them, which Bill agreed to do and reached out to his flight instructor, who also declined the opportunity to take them the 360 miles to Duluth, MN.

The owner of the ballroom was Larry Geer, who had over twenty years of experience as a pilot and warned Holly that flying in the upper Midwest darkness in sub-zero temperatures along with uncertain weather conditions would be very risky.

Holly wanted to do his laundry, as he had no clean clothes, and get some sleep, as the flight would have been less than a two-hours. The closest airport to Moorhead, MN was Hector Airport in Fargo, ND.

Originally on that flight, it was supposed to be Buddy Holly, Tommy Allsup (lead guitarist), and Waylon Jennings (bassist). After the show, Holly called his wife and Valens called his brother Robert Morales from a payphone booth that has since been locked up at the Surf Ballroom.

Carroll Anderson, with his wife and eight-year-old son, gave them a ride to the Mason City Airport.

1947 Beechcraft Bonanza Aircraft

The plane was a 1947 Beechcraft Bonanza model 35 V-Tail, which was a four-seater. Beechcrafts were made in Wichita, KS. Louis Giannola, a thirty-plus year aviation expert, noted the Bonanza was a great airplane and more performance based. They are still in manufacturing today. Those with the V-tail was called "Doctor Killer" because in that time, only doctors could afford them but did not know how to handle the airplanes and would overstress them, ripping off the tail. They need to be flown by someone with experience and not a novice. Upon research, I found reports that state there was a history of inflight problems with the 1947 Bonanza 35 V-Tail. The Beechcraft had a history of structural failures and a high incidence of in-flight failures, weight and balances problems, and control issues. From 1962-2007 the NTSB recorded an average of three V-Tail structure failures each year, which was often due to visual flight rules (VFR) into thunderstorms and icing. The narrow weight and balance problems were from loading the aircraft in the rear. The aircraft has light controls and is stable in pitch but less so when in a roll, which requires proficient pilots, especially with hand-flying (no autopilot). Early wing and center section problems were corrected beginning with the A35, which resulted in no more real occurrences.

All structure-related accidents were caused by the plane being flown outside the envelope, meaning something that is considered dangerous that could lead to the loss of control or structural damage, in which the pilot loses control. The V-Tail was said to go in a spiral dive in a heartbeat!

The engine had been overhauled forty hours before the accident, which, according to Giannola, is not a bad thing. The V-tail Beechcraft Bonanza had a wingspan of thirty-two feet ten inches, with a height of six feet, seven inches. The empty weight for this plane is 1,458 pounds, with a gross weight of 2,550 pounds, and has a maximum speed of 184 mph, with a cruising speed of 175 at ten thousand feet and could hold a maximum of forty gallons of fuel, which would last seven hundred and fifty miles.

The cost in 1959 was $36 per passenger. Dion has stated that he was asked about a seat, but he declined because he knew his parents were struggling to pay their rent, which was exactly that amount. Thirty-six dollars in 1959 is equivalent to $382 in 2024.

The Big Bopper made a deal with Waylon for his seat, which Buddy approved. There wasn't a coin flip with Jennings as some movies and stories suggest. Jennings told Richardson, "You can have my seat as long as it's okay with Buddy."

Holly went to Jennings to verify, and Waylon stated, "Yeah, that's good."

Buddy said, jokingly, "I hope your old bus freezes up."

Waylon replied in a joking manner, "I hope your old plane crashes."

This messed up Jennings for many years, as he felt he had caused the crash. Jennings also told Rolling Stone Magazine in 1973, "The only reason Buddy went on that tour was because he was broke. He didn't want to go, but he had to make some money."

The famous coin flip that has been talked about for years and seen in movies did involve Ritchie Valens. Valens was signing autographs when Tommy Allsup made a last check of the dressing room, and, according to Allsup, Ritchie said to Tommy, "You gonna let me fly?"

Allsup reached into his pocket and pulled out a fifty-cent piece, saying, "Call it!"

Valens chose heads and won the toss.

Carroll Anderson called Dwyer Flying Service Incorporated, which was located at Mason City Airport, to arrange the plane.

Mason City, Iowa is the birthplace of Meredith Wilson, the musician and playwright of The Music Man, based on the places and people of Wilson's hometown and referred to as "River City." It was one of the five longest running musicals in Broadway history, as the play was released in 1957 and the film debuted in 1962. In Mason City, you will find Music Man Square, where you can walk on the streetscape out of the movie. Located just outside the square, you will come upon a statue of Meredith Wilson, complete with his mace in one hand and tipping his hat in the other, as if he's marching in a parade.

Anderson drove the three musicians to the airport with his wife and son and even helped them load their luggage onto the plane. He shook Buddy Holly's hand and said, "I wish you only the best." He witnessed the plane take off along with Dwyer. The plane took off at 12:55 a.m. on Tuesday, February 3rd, 1959. According to the Civil Aeronautics Board (CAB), the aircraft accident report states the plane took off toward the south in a normal manner, turned, and climbed to an estimated altitude of eight hundred feet. The aircraft then headed in a northwesterly direction. When approximately five miles had been traveled, the taillight of the aircraft was seen to descend gradually until it disappeared. Following this, many unsuccessful attempts were made to contact the aircraft by radio.

Dwyer, who was the owner of the plane, was watching from a platform outside the tower, and Anderson, who was watching from the ground, both saw the taillight gradually disappear. Dwyer requested to try to reach pilot Roger Peterson but was unable to do so. The time was 1:00 a.m., which was five minutes after takeoff.

The Crash and 2015 Reexamination

The plane took off per reports between 12:55 & 12:58 a.m. and had crashed by 1:07 a.m.

The seating arrangements on the aircraft were pilot Roger Peterson and Buddy Holly in the front two seats. In the back left was JP Richardson, and Ritchie Valens sat behind Buddy Holly. According to L.J. Coon, a retired pilot and aircraft dispatcher requested the re-examination. The seating arrangements were critical to evenly balance the weight in the plane and each passenger was specifically assigned where to sit by Dwyer. Buddy Holly was 180+, Ritchie Valens 190+, & Big Bopper was 220+. Valens and Holly were instructed to sit in the back while Richardson was told to sit in the front with Pilot Peterson. As they were walking out of Dwyer Flying Service to the airplane, Holly instructed Richardson to sit in the back which infuriated Dwyer as Holly was not following his instructions. Buddy had taken flying lessons, and this would place him in front of the airplane controls.

Is this what Jerry Dwyer took with him to his grave? Knowing the plane could not handle the weight distribution with Holly in the front seat? Was this his regret that he did not stop the plane from taking off? He had mentioned that the CAB report was incorrect, and he had information to prove otherwise.

Coon stated there was a "forced landing" which means due to circumstances beyond the pilots control such as adverse weather or other issues an emergency landing is needed because the aircraft can no longer fly on its intended flight.

On February 3rd, 1959, the weather forecast called for a cold front coming from the NW corner of Minnesota all the way through central Nebraska and a secondary cold front through North Dakota. Widespread snow showers were expected ahead of the front.

The winds were so high at Mason City at the time of takeoff, one could figure they would encounter adverse weather during the flight. It was not going to be a smooth flight by any means. These gusting winds, along with very high probability of turbulence, would have caused the rate of climb indicator along with the turn and bank indicator to fluctuate to the extent that reading and understanding them would have been difficult for Pilot Peterson. This would have required a high degree of concentration and/or doing multiple things at once, which through his training says he was not adept at.

The US weather bureau issued a flash advisory of bad weather on the plane's route. Pilot Peterson never received the information, and there were no witnesses to the crash. The weather briefing mentioning adverse flying conditions should have been highlighted. If you're familiar with this piece of history, you know that there was terrible weather that night, as it was snowing and blowing. The conditions were awful— poor visibility on a cold night with snow blowing across the runway. The plane should never have been in the air and was only in the air for a few minutes before crashing into a farm field about five miles northwest of Mason City Airport. The site was covered with about four inches of snow by daybreak.

Although the plane was not in the air for very long, the flight was turbulent. Different reports state that the aircraft was headed to crash into a farmhouse northeast of Clear Lake had it not been for the owner turning on a yard light, which caused the plane to rise up, barely missing the home, barn, and a group of trees. After this close call, it headed for their neighbor's house but accelerated over the top of the roof! It crashed on the farm ground owned by Albert Juhl, and no one heard the crash. The Juhl house is located an eighth of a mile from the crash site. Albert slept through the night, but his wife did claim she heard the plane above and thought it was going to hit the house but returned to sleep. Her son, who lived next door, also heard it. The plane was obviously out of control and trying desperately to regain control, almost crashing into three different houses on its way down.

At 3:30 a.m., Fargo control tower alerted Mason City Airport that the flight never arrived. Dwyer requested an alert in Minneapolis, which was sent out at 5:16 a.m., and by 6:45 a.m., the Air Force Search and Rescue Center was contacted. The bodies lay for ten hours as snowdrifts formed around them. The wreckage was not found until 9:35 a.m. that morning after Jerry Dwyer got up in an aircraft, spotted the plane within six minutes, and called the authorities. The Mason City Globe-Gazette reported in the Wednesday February 4th edition that Dwyer could not get up in the air for several hours due to early morning fog.

The right wing hit the ground first and right-side fuselage broke off. It tore a section of ground four inches deep and three feet long, though the ground was frozen solid! The fact the aircraft struck the ground in a steep turn with the nose lowered slightly shows that there was some control that was had at impact. Once the plane hit the ground, it cartwheeled for several hundred feet before coming to rest against the barbedwire fence. Along the path from where the plane hit to where it ended up in a tangled mass and hard to recognize, as there were airplane pieces found that included parts of the instrument panel, a shoe, and a travel bag. The three singers were thrown, and the pilot was pinned inside the wreckage. The two front seat belts and the middle ones of the rear seat were torn free from their attachment points, while the two rear outside belts remained attached to their fittings. The buckle of one was broken, and none of the webbing and no belts for the occupants were broken. Keep in mind that in 1959, seat belts were not mandated and hardly worn in those days, even in automobiles. From this description, it looks like none of them were wearing them. The landing gear was still in the upright position, and the aircraft was determined to be traveling at a high speed of 165 to 170 miles per hour at impact with the ground. Pieces of the plane were found over five hundred and forty feet across the frozen cornfields.

Photographer Elwin Musser took crash photos that occurred off the intersection of 315th/Gull Ave. Early reports stated five had died, as Tommy Allsup was thought to be among the deceased, since his wallet was found in the wreckage. He had given his wallet to Holly, who put it in his coat pocket because his mother had sent him a letter that was sitting in Fargo, ND and asked Buddy to pick it up for him, which he would need identification for.

Jim Collison, who at the time of this writing was ninety-one and the only living person who was on the scene that morning as the reporter for the Globe Gazette Newspaper, expressed to me that to him, this was just another tragic story that meant nothing to him. Jim was more interested in a story he did on New Year's Eve that year, when he rode in a highway patrol car and was sent to a crash south of Mason City that took the life of a woman. He stated, "Buddy Holly meant nothing to me." Collison had five years of experience at this point with the daily newspaper and knew the names of the musicians, but that was all, as it wasn't the kind of music he liked. The call came in from the county coroner's office, so he and Elwin Musser, the photographer who took all the crash photos, headed to the location. On the way there, they assumed it was entertainers on the plane and then heard the names on the radio.

Once arriving at the scene, they had to wait for thirty minutes to be allowed to the wreckage when the coroner arrived. While they were waiting, the only other people there were the investigator from the sheriff's office, Jerry Dwyer, and the photographer from the television station. The city editor of the newspaper and the public who wanted to see did not start arriving until the afternoon and were not allowed anywhere close to where the plane crashed, which is about a quarter mile from the road.

Collison was under a time crunch to get the story written and to the Associated Press (AP) right away. He said, "I wasn't on the site more than fifteen minutes. Muss (Musser) was under more pressure to get the photos developed being it was different then and just couldn't download them. They had to be developed!" He left the Globe Gazette in 1963.

Coroner Ralph E. Smiley's M.D. report from February 3rd, 1959 states that deputy sheriff Bill McGill arrived and came upon a mass wreckage that approximated a ball, with one wing sticking up diagonally from one side. The plane was red with white and black trim. Deputy Sheriff Lowell Sandquist, who was an experienced pilot and had flown in and out of Mason City Airport, was present when the radio and navigation equipment was examined. Sanquist told the officer in charge in the tower that Peterson was to file a flight plan after getting into the air. When this was not received, attempts to reach him ended with no reply.

The Magneto switches in the cockpit were both in the off position. Giannola states, "That this is very odd." These switches are permanent magnets and coils to produce high voltage to fire the aircraft, like a sparkplug that allows the aircraft to run. The switches drive the sparkplugs in a piston aircraft. It is a dual system that creates redundancy in case you lose one cylinder bank ignition, you have still have another one. According to pilots, these being off is not good and this would have been a bad move. They could have been switched off in an emergency, but the engine would not run, and Giannola adds, "There is zero reason for this, especially during takeoff, as Peterson would have basically killed the motor.

Giannola has been studying crashes his whole career and said what could have happened is due to the force of the crash being a violent incident, anything is possible such as a knee, body part, or a briefcase could have hit it and knocked it to the off position. There was no evidence of any in-flight structural failure or failure of any of the controls. The damaged engine, which was a Continental model E185-8, was dismantled and examined, finding no evidence of any malfunctioning or failure during the flight. Both blades of the propeller were broken at the hub, meaning the engine was producing power when it hit the ground.

On many occasions, something good comes out of a bad situation, which is the case here. Within months of the crash, official protocols were put in place to ensure the names of victims of traumatic incidents are not released until families have been notified.

What could have happened with this plane?

Bad weather is said to be the cause, because the plane should not have been in the air, which is easy to understand. Pilots have said they believe the wings of the aircraft iced up and Roger Peterson could have been attempting an emergency landing and missed when his right wing hit the ground. Icing is a possibility, as, with ice, all you need on the surface of wing is the roughness of sandpaper, which would diminish fifty percent of lift.

Some of the contributing factors to the crash include serious deficiencies in the weather briefing and the pilot's unfamiliarity with the instruments. Pilot error has been stated as a cause due to the directional gyros. It is my opinion that from the momentous hours of research, Pilot Peterson may have put the throttle down, so to speak, thinking they were rising, and flew the plane right into the ground.

Carroll Anderson had to identify the bodies of the musicians. Jerry Dwyer had always said he had his own theories of what happened, but to my understanding, he didn't ever discuss them before he passed, as he received death threats after the incident and stated he had evidence that would change the CAB findings.

There is nothing in the CAB report of any fire or smell of fuel. Odds are good for a fire due to fuel, although Giannola has seen wreckage in the past where there was no post-accident fire. The weather conditions may have diluted the fuel. Investigations concluded he flew into an area of total darkness, was unable to see anything to give him a visual clue to the airplane's flight attitude, became spatially disoriented quickly, and lost control of aircraft. Spatial disorientation is the top reason for the accident according to

Giannola and could have entered what is referred to as the death spiral, as you are listening to your inner ear and not the instruments. The crash reports from CAB state that the plane was 90 degrees, which means it was on its side and rolled to the right, pitched down.

The CAB report included an attachment titled A Safety Message for Pilots. It's a summary that all pilots need to be aware that this gyro is displayed in an opposite manner. Pilots with sufficient training on both instruments are fully aware, but without this training and repetitive experience, the instinct reaction will cause an improper application, with disorientation. The pilot needs to be highly skilled in instrument training, or the period of disorientation can be fatal. The theory that Roger became confused once he flew into the darkness, adding in the reports of him having vertigo, becoming confused in the air when easily distracted, along with not being familiar with the Sperry Gyro, in my opinion is the combination for this crash.

This capitalized statement gets to the point: KNOW YOUR AIRCRAFT EQUIPMENT.

Do not rely upon any equipment under circumstances requiring its use for the safe conduct of the flight until you have acquired sufficient experience to ensure your ability to use it properly. This Beechcraft and American Airlines flight 320 both listed a misreading of instruments as well pilot error as the cause of these crashes. I find it odd that the summary was included in the crash report, as if they are saying, 'here is the cause of the crash' along with, 'it was the pilot's fault.'

Making sure everyone is aware going forward is a corrective action to avoid it occurring again, but why else would this be added?

> "This story in from Clear Lake, Iowa. Three of the agent's top rock and roll singing stars Ritchie Valens, JP "the Big Bopper" Richardson, and Buddy Holly died today with their pilot in the crash of a chartered plane following an appearance before a thousand fans in Clear Lake last night. They chartered a plane at Mason City airport and took off at twelve-fifty a.m. for Fargo, North Dakota. Their four-seat single engine plane never made it off the ground, it crashed minutes later. It skidded across the snow for some five hundred feet, and Holly, twenty-one, and Valens a seventeen-year-old recording sensation, were thrown from the wreckage. The wreckage, meanwhile, was not discovered until long after dawn. The other members of the tour, including singer Frankie Sardo, The Crickets and Dion, and the Belmont had made that trip by bus."

-Newscast about plane crash recorded on February 3rd, 1959, radio station K.L.L.L. in Lubbock, Texas

There are a few different theories on what happened to the wreckage. Some say it was taken to a storage somewhere in Mason City, Iowa, while others say it was buried, and some believe it was even destroyed. Nicholas was told a couple stories directly from Dwyer before he passed away from Alzheimer's. One time, he told him it was buried somewhere and another time he didn't know where it was. Jeff believes Dwyer had the front nose wheel, the cowling (steering wheel), and the altimeter. Dwyer repeatedly stated he was going to sell the wreckage for a million dollars for his retirement, but he never did.

Jim Collison doesn't believe the stories of the wreckage being buried or Dwyer forgetting where he buried it. His memory from some twenty-plus years ago recalled a casual conversation with Jerry, who told him the plane was in storage but wasn't telling anyone where it was. Jim said, "Knowing Jerry, I would have done the same." Although he does think at this point, it should be put on display, as people would pay a fee to view it. I agree, as it would bring millions to the Dwyer Estate. People from all over the world would come to see it, with an influx of visitors to Clear Lake/Mason City area.

If anybody out there knows where that wreckage is, please reach out. After all the research, time, and interest, to put eyes on this piece of American History would be monumental.

The plane was owned by Dwyer, who passed away in 1993. His wife Barbara passed away in 2021, and they have surviving children. One thing that Jeff Nicholas, John Mueller, Randy Brown, a longtime Iowa resident who is a devoted music fan, and I, along with more than likely many others, agree on is that the wreckage needs to be on display in Clear Lake, Iowa for everyone to see.

Questions I have always wanted to know the answers to but will not ever receive are: Why did they not wait until morning? They could have stayed in Clear Lake, got a good night's rest, food, shower, and did their laundry. Got up in the morning and with a two-hour flight still beat the bus and landed shortly after. Why didn't Jerry Dwyer go look for the plane that night? Not in the air but in a car, as he had seen approximately where it would have gone down. If the weather was that bad, where he could not have gone and searched, then the plane should have been grounded. Why didn't Dwyer fly the plane himself? Something I have pondered for a couple years, which has always been food for thought.

2015 Reexamination of Crash

The reexamination was filed on January 15th, 2015, at the request of retired pilot and aircraft dispatcher L.J. Coon from New England, who claimed the original 1959 report was inaccurate. Coon speculated the plane suffered a fuel system failure and possible malfunction of the right rudder pedal. There were different claims of what caused the crash, which caused this reexamination. He asked some great, thought provoking questions.

Who fueled the aircraft?

Why were the fuel gauges not mentioned in the original report?

Why was there no mention of ANY fuel in the wing tanks? Dwyer told Lehmer he personally filled both tanks with 80 octane gas.

There is zero mention of fuel odor, the caps being secured, of any danger from spilled fuel at the crash site, or fuel danger in general.

The weight was not evenly distributed, as Roger Peterson and Big Bopper were on one side of the plane, with Valens and Holly on the other side. Valens and JP added hundreds of pounds to the weight. This theory is the plane may have become unstable. Over forty pounds of luggage was loaded into the rear of the plane, and this, along with the weight of the fuel and the human total weight, could give the aircraft some unstable tenancies. Giannola told me, "Overweight is a possibility, being the Bonanza has a very narrow CG window, and it is a small space inside, especially for four people. Overall, the whole thing is bad."

Did Holly ask or maybe try to fly the plane once they leveled off? Another theory was that Buddy Holly accidentally pushed on the right rudder pedal. The rudder pedal controls the rotation of the vertical axis of a plane. Those in the aviation industry have told me that if Holly did turn around to talk to somebody in the back and accidentally pushed on the right rudder pedal, the plane would have tipped to the right, but by human nature, your foot would come off the pedal, causing Pilot Peterson to correct the plane, and being in bad weather, this could be possible. The National Transportation Board (NTSB) declined these stating insufficient evidence to meet the reconsideration. There are people in Iowa who believe that there was some sort of commotion on the aircraft, believing something happened on that flight that night. Holly's eagerness to fly had been documented many times, especially once in the air. Some feel he may have tried to take control of the "throwover wheel" (steering). The autopsy report on Peterson stated he had puncture wounds to the chest that are indicative of someone who was controlling the aircraft, and his right thumb was partially amputated, which could have resulted from having a death grip on the steering yolk at impact.

Thorogood believes, "Always travel by bus and stay out of the private plane!"

The Tour Continues

The rest of the members of the tour found out in their hotel lobby the next morning when they asked what rooms Holly, Valens, and Richardson were in and then heard it on the television. The tour continued the very next night, when Waylon Jennings sang Buddy's songs and then fifteen-year old Bobby Vee filled in for Holly.

Bobby, along with his older brother and a couple more friends, answered the local radio call from Fargo, ND the day after the crash to fill in for the deceased artists. Backstage, they were asked what the group name was, and they had nothing. Just moments before the curtain opened, they called themselves The Shadows.

Bobby, who was fifteen at the time, had never played before a crowd before that night in Moorhead, Minnesota. He later said he couldn't believe he did it, but that night completely changed his life forever. Vee is best known for the hit record, "Take Good Care of My Baby."

Here is an interview with Red Robinson (Red Robinson's Legends) and Bobby Vee, recorded in 1986.

Robinson: "These are the Legends of Rock. Bobby Vee got his big break filling in for Buddy Holly after his tragic accident, I asked Bobby how he felt."

Vee: "The scene for me is that my knees were knocking, and I was scared to death. It was every imaginable emotion. It was from my own stage fright to the euphoria of being on stage. When I think back on it, I don't know I'm certain that in 1986 that would never happen, that the show wouldn't go on, but I think that was part of our tradition at that point, that you know, hell or high water—the show will go on."

Robinson: "Leading up to that, had you pursued a record career on your own? I mean before obviously you were brought into the spot(light)."

Vee: "No, I was just one of those guys that used to go to all the shows that came through town. My older brother and I, he played guitar too, and we used to go to all the shows and we had a little band called "The Shadows," and the local radio station, after they heard of the tragedy, asked for local talent to help fill in, and we called the station and ended up being on stage that night, actually opening the show, and it was several, well a few months after that, there was a fellow in the audience that night that started booking us, and I'd been writing some songs and I went in and cut a song that I wrote called "Suzie Baby," and [it was] one of those crazy things, you know, whoa! You were there playing it, number one, and we started getting calls from major companies. Liberty Records, and signed [with] them in 1960."

Robinson: "Who did most of the arrangements in those days, was it Snuffy Garrett?"

Vee: "Snuffy produced all of my songs. Snuffy had been a friend of Buddy Holly. He was a disc jockey in Lubbock, Texas and had moved out to Los Angeles, and he heard "Suzie Baby" and thought 'boy, that sounds a little bit like the Crickets and Buddy Holly,' and so he signed us because of that, and I started working with Snuffy, and he produced all the records and Ernie Freeman did the arranging."

Robinson: "Bobby Vee's "Rubber Ball" was the first of a string of hits in the early 60s. Here, Bobby tells us about one of his biggest influences."

Vee: "To this day, I'm still a big Buddy Holly fan. I think that for men, anyway, a lot of people say Elvis Presley or whoever, [but] for me, Buddy Holly was the rock and roller. He never made a bad record. He was full of energy and so innovative. He wrote all his tunes. I met the Crickets when I moved to Los Angeles and started recording there. Jerry Allison the drummer played on "Rubber Ball" and a few of my things, and Sonny Curtis. Those guys were always around, and it was a natural thing; I loved their music. My music, I never really would have ever been a rock and roll singer. I'm a pop singer, but my roots were in rock and roll. Somewhere in my mind, I'm just out there screaming away, you know, with my guitar, and so that was fun for me because it gave me a chance to go do some rocking 50s rock and roll, which I love."

Robinson: "Your career spanned such an era, and I want to get to that right now, from '59 and that tragedy, you know, that took Buddy Holly's life. Your career moved forth, but you went through a lot longer period of time than a lot of the artists when the British Invasion hit. It seemed to me that Bobby Vee said, 'Okay, I'm going over to England.' It seems like you took your sound over to England, and you stayed in the charts all through it all."

Vee: "Well, I was lucky. The biggest selling record that I had of my whole career was "Coming Back When You Grow Up," which was the late 60s, but we were very fortunate through the early 60s. I had three or four records a year that were in the charts, some of them big hits and some of them were just kind of, you know, the bottom hundred, but they made it, nevertheless."

Robinson: "I saw a picture here, and I think it's out of a British publication, April 1964, and there in England with the Beatles and Dusty Springfield is Bobby Vee."

Vee: "I've never even seen this. I'd love to have a copy of this. You know, after all these years, I'm finally starting to put stuff together and say, 'Hey, that was kind of neat.' You know, it was all in a box somewhere. You know, I'd love to get a copy of this."

Buddy Holly Memorial Site

The crash site is on private farmland that can be found a quarter mile west of Gull Ave. and 315 St. It is five miles north of Clear Lake, IA.

In 1999, four trees were planted along the fence in a row for the four on aboard the aircraft. The first time Larson visited the memorial site, he had goosebumps up and down all over, as he just could not believe he was standing right there. In 1979, he visited the site with a temperature of minus sixty-five below zero with the wind chill! I'm not sure how many people outside of Larson would brave this frigid air to pay their respects. When we were talking, I mentioned that some refer to this site as sacred ground, and he immediately responded with, "You bet it is!" in a no-nonsense tone that could be felt from here to Clear Lake.

Jeff Nicholas is a farmer by trade, and Buddy has been a big part of his life. His father bought the farm in the early 60s, and as a young kid, he would pick up rocks on the farm ground with absolutely no idea that anything of any significance had happened there. It wasn't until 1979 when the local DJ "The Mad Hatter" started talking about a twenty-year party in reference to the 1959 Winter Dance Party that he learned its significance.

Ken Paquette from Wisconsin was the one who searched and identified exactly where the crash occurred. It wasn't long after the 1979 party that people started showing up to see where the plane ended up. People from all over the world and as many as two dozen at one time could be seen walking down the grass or snow-packed path to the memorial site. Couples will walk hand in hand with tears in their eyes as they recall where they were when they heard the news. There is a gravel parking lot with a small donation box right across the street from the access point to the grass walking path that is adorned with a large pair of horn-rimmed glasses. As I was talking with Jeff, there were a half-dozen cars in the lot. A local welder to the area who has since passed away constructed the signature Buddy Holly Glasses at the request of Nicholas, which were completed around the year 2000. The reason to place something at the beginning of the walking path was due to the neighbors telling Nicholas that people were knocking on their door, looking for the spot, and although they were happy to tell them, they stated it would be nice to have a direction of where to go. The glasses are great to mark the entrance, but I think they need a couple of additions, like a phone for Bopper and maybe even La Bamba for Ritchie.

When asked if people visit during the harsh weather of winter, I was told people always show up, and during the winter, there are times when the monument must be dug out from under the snow so people can see it.

One thing is clear—the passion and understanding of people who visit.

Nicholas told me the traffic has increased the last couple of years, some of it due to the 2022 documentary The Day the Music Died, but he finds it amazing how this story gets bigger and bigger the farther we get away from the time it happened.

Jeff enjoys stopping and visiting people when he sees an out of state license plate, He tells the story of one day during harvest season, when he pulled up and there was a guy from Ohio, leaning with his back against his car, and he wouldn't look at him. Jeff asked if everything was alright, the man looked up and had tears streaming down his face, and all the gentlemen could get out from being choked up was, "Lots of memories."

"Sir, you need to understand, you aren't where you think you are," he told him, because some people think the glasses are the spot. He instructed the man to walk the fence line to the memorial. He went to town, bought a camera, came back, and spent a couple hours there.

Paquette, who was from Portersfield, WI and a fan of that era, felt something needed to be at the "exact" location of the plane wreckage. In 1988, he made a stainless-steel guitar with a set of three stainless steel records. The guitar has the names of the artists etched with the date 2/3/59. The records have the titles of songs with the record label for each artist's biggest hit. "Peggy Sue" on Coral, "Donna" on Del-Fi, and "Chantilly Lace" on Mercury. Paquette made a similar memorial and placed it at the Riverside Ballroom in Green Bay, WI, where they played on February 1st, 1959. A steel monument to Roger Peterson with a pair of pilot's wings was placed in 2009, some twenty-one years after the other memorial. Paquette said, "It should have been done sooner." Peterson's memorial was unveiled by his former boss, Jerry Dwyer and his wife Barbara.

For over forty years, the master of ceremonies Bob Hale did not visit the crash site, and on that dreadful morning, he drove to the location but decided not to go to the wreckage.

As we talked, Nicholas watched people walking to the memorial site. It has recently been added to the GPS, which will more than likely add even more traffic.

While there, close your eyes, and you will hear that distinctive voice of The Big Bopper at the entrance belt out, Helloooo, Baby! Ritchie's smile hitting that guitar, singing with his young voice, 'Swing me, swing me all the way down there' as he leads you to the spot, and upon leaving, the Texas drawl of Buddy saying, 'Oh Boy, Rave On, Everyone!'

Shredded Innocence

This awful news had a profound effect on people, as they remembered where they were when they first heard about it. Stories of kids in gym class as it was announced over the school P.A. system that sent girls crying and hugging each other. The shock of this tragic plane crash was felt not only across the United States but across the world, even in England, where a young seventeen-year-old Graham Nash was in tears.

Buddy had toured overseas, and his music had reached the charts, which were heard all over the globe. Teenagers were in mourning; they were deeply hurt and felt sadness they were unable to explain. Teen Idols, who had changed the scope of their music, had left and would not be heard again. Tears were shed, and some even felt disillusioned.

On one account, I was told from a gentleman who wished to remain anonymous, "The next day in school, it was very quiet, and the halls just felt empty."

For the first time, young teens needed to find the courage to start again, as life wasn't stopping for them. They had to find a sense of being alive, and many felt more connected to one another as they all processed this news.

Clear Lake's Mayor Crabb recalled hearing the news on the car radio, as he was a freshman at Rutgers University in New Jersey. It was a Sunday evening, listening to a station from New York City with the other guys, and upon hearing the news bulletin, they all looked at each other like WHAT! Is this real'?

The families of the deceased are those who have been affected the most, and they are the ones who find peace when they visit the Surf Ballroom, but not the memorial. Maria Elena has never wanted to go to the site, but the Valens and Richardsons have and found peace in Clear Lake.

Niki Sullivan, after hearing the news, asked his mother to call Mrs. Holley to confirm it. When she answered the phone, she asked her, "Is it true what I heard about Buddy?"

She replied, "Oh, I don't know, what?"

She didn't even know! She told her she was on her way over and not to listen to the radio, but it has been said that Holly's mother then heard the news on the radio at the family home in Lubbock, screamed, and collapsed to the floor, as she had lost her youngest son. Larry Holley couldn't even turn on a radio for ten years! He later had a music room with an extensive vinyl collection from big name artists who would come through town and give him their album.

Larry's daughter, Sherry, found out the next day when her parents told her she had to go to school, as she was in the first grade. She explained like it had just happened, "I was so sad and crying all day. The teachers were asking me what's wrong? I said, "My uncle passed away." She then sat in silence for a few seconds, reliving the moment.

Everyone was simply distraught.

There was so much remorse in America, as Buddy Holly, Ritchie Valens, and JP Richardson were looked at as leaders of that generation, but they had now perished.

As Red Robinson puts it, "I can still picture that day when the news came across the wire. I reached for a current Holly hit from the KGW hit rack and put my hands on his 'It Doesn't Matter Anymore.' The significance of that title leaped into my heart. It was a sign off for Buddy's career."

Many who knew Valens or knew of him just could not believe that he was killed, it was devastating. Many were sad for years afterward, especially those from Ritchie's hometown, as this was their guy who was on his way to stardom.

Rocha said, "Not Ritchie! No!" He ran out of work to the Valens home to give Ritchie's mother, Connie, a hug and a kiss. Keane felt like he'd lost his own son, as he was Ritchie's legal guardian for travel purposes.

Concha blamed herself over and over because she let Ritchie go. Keane couldn't leave California, so he hired an adult travel companion for Valens, but after the first few stops, he was gone due to how miserable the tour was. By this time, though, there was a camaraderie between the guys, as they all took care of one another.

Gail Smith was told by the principal of the junior high school that Ritchie had died. He was aware they were close friends and found her at recess. He placed his arm around Gail and took her to the side and broke the news. She fainted, and he held her.

Smith said, "It was exceptionally difficult to pick up and move on. The whole school became different, as the entire era had changed. It was no longer fun."

She was home for two weeks and stayed in bed for a week. After the funeral, her mother and her always went to the Valens' home and only came home to sleep, as they lived just two short blocks away. They would arrive first thing in the morning and stay until Concha wanted to go to bed. They prayed a lot and played Ritchie's music constantly. Concha asked Gail to take care of the flowers and messages, as the whole house was filled. She remembers the first one coming from Eddy Arnold, and ones from Colonel Parker, Elvis, and even Roy Orbison. A couple of weeks later, the principal gave her the tapes from the assembly that he'd taped by having it piped into his office's speaker for the P.A. system and placing a tape recorder in front of it. Keane had to clean it up quite a bit to what is heard today.

Bingham recalled vividly the news. He received a call early in the morning from Norman Petty and asked if he had seen the news. He had just woken up and had not. Petty instructed him to turn the TV on, which he did, as it kept repeating that Buddy, Ritchie, and the Big Bopper were killed in an airplane crash. Petty asked him to get dressed and come down to the studio because the phones were ringing off the wall. Bingham went down and spent all day on the phone talking to people. It really was devastating, because three months earlier they had been on tour with them, and it took the air out of them.

Larson told the vivid detail of learning that his idol had been killed. He was walking down the hall on the second floor of the high school, when a friend of his came running out of this room and said, "Hey, Don, did you hear the news? Buddy Holly, The Big Bopper, and Ritchie Valens got killed in a plane crash."

Larson looked at him and replied, "Hey, man, why would you say something like that?"

The answer was, "Because it's true."

Don didn't believe him and went to his afternoon class for radio and television, which had a little control room in it. In there was a radio, so he turned it on, and a song by The Big Bopper was playing. Once it was over, the disc jockey said, "That was another song by the late great Big Bopper." His heart sank into his stomach, and he was in shock. He went home after school and did something he had not done ever before—skipping dinner with his parents. He went into his room, shut the door, and didn't come out until breakfast the next morning. Don played their music all night.

Lasting Legacy

Every day, there are musicians all over the world, dreaming of making it big, and the vast majority of them will fade away into the sunset. Those who are discovered will have their opportunity at possible stardom, while others who were passed over may find a new way to be seen, as Holly, Valens, and Richardson did. Each of them in their own way. Holly found Petty, Keane found Valens, and Richardson found a telephone. Few will stand out in a crowd. Buddy paved the way for countless rock and roll stars.

Ritchie was just seventeen. Seventeen! Yet he is still unforgettable. Their deaths left a huge hole in those who liked and loved them along with their music. The success each felt was not without some frustration and at times even feeling discouraged.

Today, the songs they left behind have stood the test of time and sustain the approval of the next generation that somehow stumble upon them.

"When you listen to a Buddy Holly song, you can't me be mad at the same time," said Don Larson.

As I have stated, 50s music puts a smile on your face. The Beatles modeled themselves after the Crickets, and John Lennon, who did not have good eyesight at all, wore glasses on stage after seeing Buddy wearing them.

Larson was in the inner circle of the Holley family, as he knew all of them. He told me, "They were such wonderful people." He truly feels he knew Buddy, as he could not have been much different than his mom, dad, and brothers. On one of his trips to Lubbock, TX for a Buddy Holly Tribute, they were all in one room at the Villa Inn, and he tells this story through tears of how he was asked to go outside by Mrs. Holley, as she wanted to speak with Don. Once outside, she looked him in the eyes and told him, "I can't thank you enough for what you have done for our son." She went on to say that she had heard he was going on radio, television, and talking with people all over the world. She explained that she and Mr. Holley were just too old and couldn't do that. "We don't have the time." At that point, Don knew he had their blessing and made them proud.

Songs have been written and recorded since this tragic day, and some of relevance include "Three Stars" by Tommy Dee in 1959 and "Tribute to Buddy Holly" by Mike Berry in 1961. Both can be found on my podcast show, Before the Lights episode, The Last Dance Party, and on Silhouette Music vinyl "The Day the Music Died." Waylon did a tribute song to Buddy called, "Old Friend." (1976) and in 1978, he recorded the single, "A Long Time Ago" with a lyric of 'Don't ask me who I gave my seat to on that plane. I think you already know. I told you that a long time ago.'

What we need today are multiple artists/groups to cover the songs from the catalogs of The Big Bopper, Ritchie Valens, and Buddy Holly. Expose these songs to not only this generation but future ones that are not familiar with this extensive collection of hit records, sharing these timeless hits. You may be surprised that you have already heard many of them. Larson said that if current artists cover Buddy Holly's songs, they shouldn't jazz them up but play them as they are. Buddy's songs are hard to duplicate because of how Buddy played them, which Townsend feels is a reason artists have not covered them. With that said, Tommy and his band in September of 2024 out of nowhere started playing Holly's

"Well...All Right," which is a track that drummer Allison only played the cymbal on. Townsend's drummer has modernized the song with drums, and Tommy stated it is so much fun to play! One is great, but we need many others to join in.

When I asked Thorogood about cover songs, he told a story back in 1968 when he skipped school, which he never did. His oldest brother John had a record called, "The Buddy Holly Story," with Buddy on the cover wearing a cashmere sweater, looking very handsome. He listened to this record all day long, sitting alone in the house, and figured out every song on the record with his guitar. He chose a few songs that he felt would make good cover songs for an artist and told his friends, who were all into The Doors and Jimi Hendrix, about putting a band together to cut these tracks, and they thought he was out of his mind. Soon after, Linda Ronstadt beat him to it, as she released "That'll Be the Day" and "It's So Easy." He went on to say that record companies aren't enthusiastic about covers because they didn't write the song and the managers, record companies, and producers get a piece of original material, so they aren't big on them and steer away from it.

Regardless of how much money they are receiving, these catalogs should be redone by today's musicians. I have an idea to help get these songs exposed, and hopefully from this book, it can now move forward.

Sherry Holley adds her name to the list of us who would like to see a current artist(s) cover songs from these rock and roll icons. She thinks it would be fabulous for a rock and roller or blues artist to do a song or two, which would build excitement. Her mosaic artwork of Buddy's glasses is beautiful and meticulously put together. She has even in the past made a lifesize acoustic guitar and used Buddy's fishing line for the strings. Buddy is talked about more now than ever, which Sherry says is due to The Buddy Holly Hall and Buddy Holly Center in Lubbock, TX.

Talking with the next generations who do not know who these rock and roll icons were, I asked a person in their thirties, "Who is Buddy Holly?"

They immediately answered, "Ooh wee hoo, I look just like Buddy Holly," which are lyrics from a track by the group Weezer in 1994. They were aware he died in a plane crash but did not know where this occurred and had no idea where Clear Lake was located. Yes, they'd heard of La Bamba but did not know the name Ritchie Valens or The Big Bopper and when asked who was in the plane with Holly, they answered that Sam (Sammy Davis Jr.), the guy from the Rat Pack.

Exactly my point on why we need these catalogs made current again.

Go make yourself a playlist of these three and enjoy their music. From the lyrics of "American Pie" by Don McLean, the music didn't die on February 3rd,1959, It's still here. What died were legends in the music industry whose memories remain alive!

Nicholas is not surprised people are still talking about this story and believe it's never going to end, as it reverberates from generation to generation. This was the dawn of a new era in our country, with culture and society changing so drastically. He said, "The glasses have come in and out of style several times. Collison, like others, is not surprised and told me he had recently spoken to someone in their eighties asking questions about the conspiracy stories.

John Mueller is doing his part and a whole lot more. Your Buddy John, as he is known, has entertained people all over North America with his highly acclaimed Winter Dance Party, the official tribute to Buddy Holly, Ritchie Valens, and the Big Bopper.

"I've never endorsed anyone doing Buddy, but I was really impressed with John... John is the only one who does it exactly like Buddy did. He's a great musician in his own right."

~*Maria Elena Holly*

When asked, when was the first time he heard the name Buddy Holly, Mueller, who has been playing Holly longer than Buddy was alive, told me this story. He was a paperboy and heard the song by Don McLean, "American Pie" with the line, "with every newspaper I delivered," and thought, Hey, I deliver newspapers. So he asked his other brothers, as they were ten to twelve years older than John, what the song meant. He was told it was about Buddy Holly, and he received handme-down records of Chuck Berry, Jerry Lee Lewis, and Holly. It was something about that music that intrigued him to pick up a guitar and try and figure out what Buddy was doing. This started the evolution of Mueller, and it was signed, sealed, and delivered after seeing the movie, The Buddy Holly Story with actor Gary Bussey playing Holly. Mueller knew he was destined to be an entertainer, and he was in love with this music.

After audiences see his show, he receives all types of feedback, as some tell him it was a healing experience, while others state they felt young again. One lady in Green Bay, WI, told him she loved the show! With so much sadness, seeing John's show helps them remember times before the crash. Mueller said playing on the same stages that the Winter Dance Party performed, such as the Riverside Ballroom in Green Bay, WI and the Surf, has bought some chilling moments, as out of nowhere, their tuners stop working. The crowds are into history and appreciate that he is keeping the music going. After a show at the Surf around one a.m., which would have been the time the plane crashed, they decided to visit the memorial site on a freezing cold winter night that felt eerie and lonely. Mueller said, "There is a definitely a vibe there."

All the families have endorsed what John has been doing. The first person Mueller met was Nikki Sullivan, who was one of the original Crickets, and he welcomed John and told him many stories, such as when they were around fourteen or fifteen years old and Buddy had a laser-like focus and knew what he wanted. Holly's brother Travis became teary-eyed after watching the tribute show and said it had brought back the essence of Buddy. John was not only surprised by this comment but he himself became teary-eyed.

From everything John knows, Buddy was a straightforward Texan and sincere guy. He stated, "Buddy was a young man who pioneered what we think of today as a rock and roll band. An innovator with music, and what sticks out the most is he was the working-class rock and roller." All stemming from one song and a movie that he watched by himself, and now John is the one who people come to see.

Thorogood agrees that Holly, Valens, and Richardson were innovators to what rock and roll music is today, as he didn't even pick up a guitar until he was twenty years old and said, "Hey, man, they were WAY ahead of me!"

Although nobody will ever know where they would have gone with their careers, George admits the talent was there, and like him, we can all imagine what would have been.

Thorogood isn't surprised this story is still being talked about over sixty-five years later, as it is a mystery with a tragic ending. He expressed that the interest is going to be there, as well as the 'what could have been' factor. He remarked, "It's an interesting story. The Beatles idolized the Crickets, and the Stones redid 'Not Fade Away.' There will be big interest forever, and the music is really damn good."

This interview between Alan Freed, a DJ who produced and promoted concerts to bring awareness to rock and roll music across North America, and Buddy Holly from October 2nd, 1958, on WNEW-TV-New York City is a little eerie.

Freed: "The one and only Buddy Holly! How are you, Buddy?"

Holly: "Fine."

Freed: "Good to see you, ole Buddy again. Where are the other fellas?"

Holly: "They're running around somewhere."

Freed: "I guess I haven't seen you since our tour, have I?"

Holly: "About in April wasn't [it]?"

Freed: "I think somewhere around there. What have you been doing and where have you been?"

Holly: "We haven't been working all summer, Alan. We just been kind of loping and taking it easy and running around some. Enjoying what we hadn't enjoyed for the whole year previously, you know, all the work going on."

Freed: "Boy, you worked hard that year."

Holly: "We're getting ready to start some new work now."

Freed: "You going on tour again?"

Holly: "I think so."

Freed: "Buddy, we had lot of fun, and we did a lot of flying."

Holly: "Yeah, we sure did. You know, I was just in town the other day in Cincinnati. Remember when we landed there, and the helicopter crashed that day?"

Freed: "That's right."

Holly: "We took the ride in there from the airport, and it reminded me of when we landed."

Freed: "I think we rode every kind of airplane imaginable."

Holly: "We sure did! (laughs)"

Freed: "Those DC 3s were really something. Boy oh boy, without the seat belts, we'd have been right through the top, that's for sure. Buddy, we had a lot of fun together, and I hope we're going to have a lot of fun together in the future too, because you're just a wonderful guy. Let's get together soon and thank you so much for being with us."

Holly: "Thank you, Alan, it has been my pleasure."

Freed: "Here is his brand new Brunswick (label) record, 'It's so Easy.'"

This music is too amazing to die, pure and simple. It will put a smile on your face and lift your spirits. It's a time capsule. People across our globe will tell you how someone becomes more of a legend after they have died. Stories start to come from all different angles, with some being true, others false, and the ones that are true become embellished. By watching any of the footage that was preserved and released, it is easy to see that Holly, Valens, and Richardson loved to perform. Holly was laser focused and created a sound that is all his own, which is still relevant to this day and paved the way for future musicians. Valens, with no musical background, came from poverty and built his own identity, while Richardson used his outgoing personality as a disc jockey to market his records. As I like to say, you are never too old to start something and always too young to quit.

Holly, the rocker who has never grown old, Valens, and Richardson all had a youthful, energetic, musical spirit that they not only carried with them but shared with audiences each time they took a stage. Nothing was forced; they were just having fun playing music that moved patrons in ways that had only been felt by Elvis Presley. Ask any person who grew up during this time about the music of the late fifties and watch their faces light up with joy as they immediately recall how that music made them feel. It's a deep spirit that lives inside each one of them that easily surfaces when a song comes on. This is the lasting legacy of the fifties, but the sounds and memories, as Buddy Holly said, will not fade away. The music of today can be traced back to Holly in some fashion. He WAS the innovator and reason for the growth of rock and roll.

"I play Buddy Holly every night before I go on; that keeps me honest."

"Buddy Holly was a huge influence on me. His songs were so simple yet so perfect. He showed me that you didn't have to be complicated to be great."

~**Tom Petty** (Rolling Stone Magazine, 2007)

"Buddy Holly was a pioneer. His approach to songwriting and recording was revolutionary, and he set the stage for so many of us who followed."

~**Joe Walsh**

Richard Zimmerman saw the Winter Dance Party in Duluth, MN and was inspired to become a rock and roller. You may know him better by his stage name, Bob Dylan. Keith Richards, the legendary guitarist of The Rolling Stones, has spoken about how Buddy Holly had a big influence on his musical career. He mentioned that Holly's playing and appearance made a big impression on him and the Stones. Richards has expressed how Holly's pioneering work shaped the course of rock and roll history. Mick Jagger, the lead singer of The Rolling Stones, said in an interview, "To English people, he was an enormous inspiration... because he was a songwriter, which Elvis wasn't. And he wrote very simple songs, sort of lesson one in songwriting. Great songs, which had simple changes and nice melodies and changes of tempo and all that. You could learn from Buddy Holly how to write songs, the way he put them together. He was a beautiful writer" (August 14th, 2014: Rolling Stones Data).

In a 2008 interview during the Crickets' induction into the Musicians Hall of Fame, Richards stated, "Without them [Buddy Holly and the Crickets], you probably wouldn't have the Beatles, and you wouldn't have the Stones" (February 12th, 2020, Legacy.com).

Paul McCartney has frequently acknowledged Buddy Holly's profound influence on not only his musical career but that it shaped The Beatles direction. In a 1985 interview for a BBC film, The Real Buddy Holly Story, McCartney expressed, "I've always loved Buddy's music; he's been a big influence on me" (By Rafael Polcaro, February 22nd, 2022: rockandrollgarage.com). McCartney, on Holly's impact on The Beatles from a songwriting approach, stated, "We didn't know people didn't write their own things... Buddy was a big influence"(by Ross Tanenbaum, December 9th, 2022: cheetsheet.com).

John Lennon openly acknowledged Buddy Holly's significant influence on his musical career. In The Beatles Anthology, Lennon stated, "Buddy Holly was the first one that we were really aware of in England who could play and sing at the same time—not just strum but actually play the licks" (Aaron Krerowicz, March 6th, 2014).

George Harrison, the renowned guitarist of The Beatles, in a 1974 interview, reflected on Holly's impact, stating, "I think one of the greatest people for me was Buddy Holly because, first of all, he sang, wrote his own tunes, was a guitar player, and he was very good–exceptionally good" (Arun Starkey, June 15th, 2023, Far Out Magazine).

They were all on a path for bigger careers in the entertainment world. In an industry that has its share of bigger than life egos, these young men were raw, unguarded, and just wanted to sing their songs in front of screaming teenagers. As the lyrics from "American Pie" tell us, "I knew if I had my chance that I could make those people dance and, maybe, they'd be happy for a while." All one has to do is put a 50s record on a turntable, and Don McLean's line comes true, because you will be happy, and it will make you dance. He asks us, "Do you believe in rock 'n' roll?" If you are reading this, then you most certainly do. "Where I'd heard the music years before. But the man there said the music wouldn't play." All this about The Day the Music Died, but you see, when you listen to the music from long ago, not only is it recognizable in the first few seconds, but you also know the song before the first word is sung. YOU are the man making the music play, and therefore it will always be alive!

Jackson Browne has a deep admiration for Buddy Holly, as he had an effect on his musical style. In a 2011 interview, Browne reflected on Holly's legacy, stating, "February 3rd, 1959 was not the day the music died, it was the day the music became immortal."

Drummer Jerry Allison quoted at one time that he and Buddy used to sit around and try to figure out how they could make it. Let me tell Buddy, Jerry, Ritchie, and JP one thing…You ALL made it!

Memories will Rave On!

Acknowledgements

I have so many people who are deserving of a thank you and to be listed in this book.

To my grandparents, who made it feasible for my parents to meet one day. You all paved the way in some fashion the standards by which my siblings and I were raised. Your memories and love live on through us all.

My parents: Words are not enough to express what they have done and meant to me. I'm the man I am because of my father. A man wise beyond his years, and although he may not have thought I was learning from him at five feet, I was, from a distance, by just observing. He left us way too soon, and he saved my life (that's another story), and for that, I'm beyond grateful and thankful. I'm proud to be named after him. I love you, Pops!

My mother: Wow! The most beautiful soul in this world. Her love, nurturing, and guidance are sometimes hard to comprehend. Many think she is my sister, as she looks nothing or acts close to her age. I simply cannot put my feelings for you into words. I love you and thank you for the ten thousand page list of things you have done for me. Dad may have made me the man that I am, but you have molded me into the person I am!

Tim, my brother, and Jen, my sister. Thank you for always supporting the list of things I have done, from being a DJ to a basketball coach to an inspirational speaker and so on and so on. Tim, your driving success is commendable. I admire you and appreciate you connecting me to people for this project. Jen, you are the doctor of the family, and your passion for your family, friends, and career is a unique quality you have. The summer vacation with you and Mom was full of daily announcements and great stops that started this all when we added Clear Lake, IA.

To all my nieces, nephews, and cousins: Kayla Hall, Marissa Malnar, Chris Canale, Katelyn Canale, my great nieces Reagan and Amilia, great nephew Carson, Missy Daugherity and her sons Breven and Dylan. I love you all!

Michelle Davies: From the first day, you have seen something in me and always let me know that I could do anything. Your support of endless logos, graphics, and helping me with my frustration with technology. You are a special human being. Thank you!

Antonino D'Ambrosio: Fratello! My brother from another mother. What can I say, you are a beautiful person. Working with you on our docuseries, interviewing you numerous times, our phone calls, your guidance and support—it's unmatched and only understandable by two Italianos. I am humbled that you agreed to write the foreword for this book, which is another piece of your beautiful work, not to mention all the assistance in bringing this to life! Love you, brother, and thank you.

To all my listeners of the podcast Before the Lights who are reading this book. Your continued support is appreciated.

Kelly Burgin: you have gone from a loyal listener to a friend and are a sensational sign maker. My gratitude for your gracious work on the book cover and beyond cannot be put into words. Thank you for all the art pieces you have sent me over the years, especially the surf ballroom and signs of the intersection of the crash site. Readers: Need a sign, please go check out K Burgin Designs.

Randy Brown (aka Mr. Concert): little did I know from a conversation at the final four in Phoenix that I was talking to someone who lived in IA. You were energized to help me find the wreckage and became a tremendous advocate in getting this book completed. A music historian, friend, and travel partner. THANK YOU! The sights, sounds, and discoveries were simply invaluable. Your assistance, dedication, and time, including countless hours of conversations about this story, coach speak, and quick stops for a hoop photo have been monumental to me.

This book would not be possible if it were not for the following people who deserve to be listed for their time and talking with me:

Gilbert Rocha, for the priceless conversation about Ritchie, who was destined for stardom.

Red Robinson, the master of interviews, who interviewed every big music star and was a star himself. Your generosity to use your interviews from The Day the Music Died is tremendously appreciated. RIP, Red.

Louis Giannola, or the aviation expert! Your insight, time, and experience were not only invaluable, but this book would not have the intricate details it now offers.

Jeff Nicholas, for our conversation that charged me up, your assistance to others, and the stories that I was excited to hear and knew others would enjoy as well. Your generosity is not taken lightly.

Thank you, Gail Smith, for reliving some difficult times and many happy times with me, as I can tell how much this has affected you.

Anthony Garcia Music for graciously allowing me to use your interview with Jape's best friend, Jerry Boynton.

Devon Gardner with Insight Mgt. for setting up my interview with Thorogood.

To George Thorogood, I appreciate the time you took during the sound check for your concert that evening in Colorado Springs. The black shades and rocker patterned jacket were awesome. Rock on!

Laurie Lietz, executive director of the Surf Ballroom, for your assistance in reaching out to the short list of people who attended the WDP.

Jim Collison, the only person alive who was on the scene that morning. Your time was priceless, and I enjoyed the conversation.

Don Larson, the biggest Buddy Holly Fan I know. Thank you for the conversations, information, and insight into the Holley family. Your knowledge is priceless.

To a friend of mine who was a guest on my podcast a couple times, and as Waylon said, "He's a good Georgia Boy!" Tommy Townsend. You were kind enough to tell me what you knew from being a protégé of Jennings and your friendships with the Crickets.

Mary Charlson, John Wonsmos, and Dilla (Niederfrank) Arneson, some of the last people still alive who were at the Surf on February 2nd, 1959. Your insight into that night's show was invaluable, and I enjoyed talking with all of you.

Ron Skinner for curating the tour of the Norman Petty Studio.

Kenneth Broad and Family: My fellow hometown native and Norman Petty Guide—thank you! Your stories and insight left Randy and I overloaded and speechless. From one bulldog to another, playing "My Hometown WIZZ" in the studio will not be forgotten.

Sherry Holley, your spirit, stories, and assistance are greatly appreciated. Keep making mosaics and singing Uncle Buddy's timeless classics.

To The Buddy Holly Center: ALL of you are wonderful people! Your welcoming hospitality and spirit are a breath of fresh air in today's world.

John Mueller aka Your Buddy John. Thank you for your time on zoom, the connections you made for me and tickets to see your EXCELLENT Winter Dance Party Show!

Appendix A

Buddy Holly's fingerprint spreads across several decades on rock and roll. He has been credited as a source of inspiration for over 100 musicians, some are listed here.

(Alphabetically by last name)

Paul Anka

Jeff Beck

David Bowie

Jackson Browne

T-Bone Burnett

Glen Campbell

Johnny Cash

Nick Cave

Alex Chilton

Eric Clapton

Elvis Costello

Marshall Crenshaw

Rivers Cuomo

Rick Danko

Dave Davies

Ray Davies

Tom DeLonge

Dion DiMucci

Bob Dylan

Steve Earle

Dave Edmunds

John Fogerty

Peter Frampton

Jackson C. Frank

Billy Fury

Art Garfunkel

Ben Gibbard

David Gilmour

Emmylou Harris

George Harrison

Levon Helm

Chris Hillman

Bruce Hornsby

Chrissie Hynde

Mark Knopfler

Nick Lowe

Jeff Lynne

Mick Jagger

Waylon Jennings

Billy Joel

Elton John

Ronnie Hawkins

Kevn Kinney

Buddy Knox

John Lennon

Kenny Loggins

Lyle Lovett

Stephen Malkmus

Brian May

Paul McCartney

Roger McGuinn

Don McLean

John Mellencamp

Colin Meloy

George Michael

Joni Mitchell

Keith Moon

Morrissey

Van Morrison

Graham Nash

Rick Nelson

Mike Nesmith

Roy Orbison

Graham Parker

Carl Perkins

Linda Perry

Tom Petty

John Prine

Cliff Richard

Keith Richards

Robbie Robertson

Linda Ronstadt

Richie Sambora

Paul Simon

Bruce Springsteen

Paul Stanley

Rod Stewart

Stephen Stills

Joe Strummer

James Taylor

The Beach Boys

The Beatles

The Everly Brothers

The Hollies

The Rolling Stones

The Who

Alex Turner

Ritchie Valens

Jimmie Vaughan

Bobby Vee

Gene Vincent

Joe Walsh

Bob Weir

Paul Weller

Steve Winwood

Ronnie Wood

(List compiled by Randy Brown, Fort Dodge, IA)

Appendix B

Songs Mentioned in Shadows Over Clear Lake

*-songs not available on Spotify

1948

"Did You Go Sailing" (Down by the River of Memories) by T. Texas Tyler-*

1952

"Salty Dog Rag" by Red Foley-*

1954

"Mood Indigo" by The Norman Petty Trio-*

1955

"Hot Rod Lincoln" by Charlie Ryan

1956

"Be-Bop-a-Lula" by Gene Vincent

"Blue Days Black Nights" by Buddy Holly and the Crickets

"Brown Eyed Handsome Man" by Chuck Berry

"It Doesn't Matter Anymore" by Buddy Holly

"It's So Easy" by Buddy Holly

"Not Fade Away" by Buddy Holly

"Raining in My Heart" by Buddy Holly

"Reddy Teddy" by Buddy Holly and the Crickets

"See You Later Alligator" by Bill Haley and His Comets

"Send Me Some Lovin'" by Buddy Holly and the Crickets

"Think It Over" by Buddy Holly

"Well...Alright" by Buddy Holly and the Crickets

1957

"All Shook Up" by Elvis Presley

"At the Hop" by Danny and the Juniors

"Beggar To a King" by Jape Richardson

"Caravan" by Henri Rose-*

"Everyday" by Buddy Holly

"I'm Gonna Love You Too" by Buddy Holly

"Lucille" by Little Richard

"Maybe Baby" by Buddy Holly and the Crickets

"Moondreams" by Buddy Holly and the Crickets

"Oh, Boy!" by The Crickets

"Peggy Sue" by Buddy Holly and the Crickets

"That'll be the Day" by Buddy Holly and the Crickets

"Susie Q" by Dale Hawkins

"You Send Me" by Sam Cooke

1958

"16 Candles" by The Crests

"Chantilly Lace" by The Big Bopper

"Classroom" by Frankie Sardo

"Come On, Let's Go" by Ritchie Valens

"Donna" by Ritchie Valens

"Fake Out" by Frankie Sardo

"Framed" by Ritchie Valens

"From Beyond" by Ritchie Valens

"Gotta Travel On" by Billy Grammer

"I Wonder Why" by Dion and the Belmonts

"La Bamba" by Ritchie Valens

"Little Red Riding Hood" by The Big Bopper

"Maybelline" by Gene Vincent

"Oh Carol" by Chuck Berry

"Ooh, My Head" by Ritchie Valens

"Purple People Eater" by Sheb Wooley

"Rave On" by The Crickets

"Rockin' Robin" by Bobby Day

"Summertime Blues" by Eddie Cochran

"That's My Little Susie" by Ritchie Valens

"The Purple People Eater Meets the Witch Doctor" by The Big Bopper

"True Love Ways" by Buddy Holly

"Volare" by Dean Martin

"We Belong Together" by Ritchie Valens

"Whole Lotta Shakin' Goin' On" By Jerry Lee Lewis

"Witch Doctor" by Ross Bagdasrian

"White Lightning" by The Big Bopper

1959

"A Teenager in Love" by Dion and the Belmonts

"Battle of New Orleans" by Johnny Horton

"Hippy Hippy Shake" by Chan Romero

"Three Stars" by Tommy Dee-*

1960

"Rubber Ball" by Bobby Vee

"Running Bear" by Johnny Preston

"Wheels" by The String-A-Longs

"When the Bells" Stop Ringing by Frankie Sardo

1961

"Ooby Dooby" by Roy Orbison

"Tribute to Buddy" Holly by Mike Berry

"Twist and Shout" by The Isley Brothers

1962

"Suzie Baby" by Bobby Vee

"Take Good Care of My Baby" by Bobby Vee

1963

"Sugar Shack" by Jimmy Gilmer and The Fireballs

1964

"You've Lost That Loving Feeling" by The Righteous Brothers

1965

"I Got You Babe" by Sonny and Cher

1966

"I Fought the Law" by Bobby Fuller Four

1967

"Come Back When You Grow Up" by Bobby Vee

1971

"American Pie" by Don McLean

Hot Rod Lincoln by Commander Cody and His Lost Planet Airman

1975

"Boogie With Stu" by Led Zepplin

1976

"Old Friend" by Waylon Jennings

1978

"A Long Time Ago" by Waylon Jennings

1994

"Buddy Holly" by Weezer

Listen to all these songs in Spotify by simply searching the playlist: Shadows Over Clear Lake or scan the code.

Bibliography

- Aircraft Accident Report, Civil Aeronautics Board, September 23, 1959
- Betts, Stephan L. Flashback: How Waylon Jennings Survived the Day the Music Died, Rolling Stone Magazine, February 3, 2015
- Blanas, Frank, The King of Clovis, Rollercoaster Books, 2014
- Collison, Jim, Four Killed In Clear Lake Plane Crash, Mason City Globe Gazette, February 4, 1959
- Coon, L.J., Reexamination of Mason City Accident February 3, 1959, N3794N,, January 15, 2015
- DiMucci, Dion, The True Buddy Holly Story, Dion, 2015
- Flannagan, S., Bruce Springsteen Used To Listen To This Rock Legend Before His Shows, grunge.com, February 23, 2022
- Freed, Alan, Interview with Buddy Holly, Music Across North America, WNEW-TV, New York City, NY, October 2, 1958
- Garcia, Anthony, Jerry Boynton Interview, Anthony Music, 2024-https://www.youtube.com/@nthonymusic
- Hiatt, Brian, Grammy Preview: Tom Petty, Rolling Stone Magazine, February 8, 2007
- Krerowicz, Aaron, The Influence of Buddy Holly on the Beatles, Aaron Krerowicz Flip Side Beatles, March 16, 2014
- Legacy Staff, Who Influenced The Rolling Stones?, legacy.com, February 12, 2020
- Lehmer, Larry, The Day the Music Died: The Last Tour of Buddy Holly, the Big Bopper, and Ritchie Valens., Schirmer Trade Books, 1977

- Long, Corey, Come on baby, just rock, rock, rock! The Inspired life and enduring legacy of Ritchie Valens, Independently published, 2024
- McCool James, and Garabedian, The Winter Dance Party Tapes: Frankie Sardo, Blue Days Productions, 2015
- McLean, Don, Buddy Holly-Rave On: The Story of Buddy Holly Documentary, Eagle Rock Entertainment, 2017
- Morales, Bob, Project Coda 25 Years After La Bamba, KMVT, 2009
- Newscast, KGLO Radio Mason City, IA, February 3, 1959 ➢ Newscast, KLLL Radio Lubbock, TX, February 3, 1959
- Polcaro, Rafael, The 3 musicians that Paul McCartney said that inspired him the most, rockandrollgarage.com, February 22, 2022
- Robinson, Red, Bobby Vee, Red Robinson's Legends, June 20, 1986
- Robinson, Red, Roy Orbison Meets Buddy Holly, Red Robinson's Legends, 2021
- Robinson, Red, Jerry Allison, Red Robinson's Legends, 2022
- Robinson, Red, Buddy Holly-Georgia Auditorium, Red Robinson's Legens, 1957
- Sonaglioni, Marcelo, Rolling Stones Quotes -Mick Jagger and Keith Richards on Buddy Holly, Rolling Stones Data, 2024
- Smiley, Ralph E., Coroner's Autopsy Reports, Coroner's of Cerro Gordo County Report, February 4, 1959
- Smiley, Ralph E., Coroner's Report of Investigation Air Crash, Coroner's of Cerro Gordo County Report, February 4, 1959

➢ Starkey, Arun, George Harrison explains why Buddy Holly was "one of the greatest people", Far Out Magazine, June 15, 2023

➢ Tannebaum, Ross, The Beatles: Why Buddy Holly Was a Significant Influence for the Fab Four, Showbiz Cheat Sheet, December 9, 2022

➢ Valens, Ritchie, Ritchie Valens in concert at Pacoima Jr. High, Del-FI Records, Inc., 1960

➢ Wohlrabe, Brooke, Sister reflects on Ritchie Valens' life, legacy, Sentinel, August 14, 2019

About the Author

Tommy Canale is an Illinois native from the small town of Streator. Although he hails from a small town, his experience is big, and he now resides in Las Vegas, Nevada. He has a vast background as an on-air radio personality, owning a mobile disc jockey business for over fifteen years, and most recently hosting his Before the Lights podcast, which is heard in over 100 countries. Tommy's guests included professional athletes, musicians, actors, and former members of organized crime families. He is the host of the Jim Feist Handicapping Show.

As a cancer survivor who was given a three percent chance to survive, his inspirational story captivates audiences across the country, as he inspires people to inspire others. After this battle, Tommy was at the helm of the Illinois Valley Community College men's basketball team, along with serving as the school's athletic director, which segued to become the National Scout Director for RecruitLook since 2014. Tommy has long been known for his creative mind, and in 2023 he wrote, developed, and put into place Stardust Trivia.

Music has always been a major part of his life since he was a young boy growing up around his family's amusement and jukebox business. To this day, you can find him listening to a vinyl record from his extensive collection.